A Noble Gift

A Butterton Brides Christmas Novella
Book 4

Ann Elizabeth Fryer

Copyright © October 10, 2024 by Ann Elizabeth Fryer

All rights reserved.

No portion of this book may be reproduced in any form without written permission from the publisher or author, except as permitted by U.S. copyright law.

AI was not used in the creation of this product.

Merry Christmas, dear readers! May you know the deep joy of God's love...

Chapter One

November 20, 1811

Bath, England

Cold and raining. A perfectly glum outlook for the day's outing. Candles flickered on either side of the mirror before me, offering little light as I turned my auburn hair this way and that. My curls wouldn't hold in this weather. The knot felt lopsided, but I didn't have the heart to call Lila back to redo my chignon. What did it matter? My hair would be tucked within a bonnet, out of sight.

"Cassandra!" Mother's voice echoed down the hall, anxious for us to be about our business.

"Coming!" A tap-tapping pecked at the window as the rain mixed with sleet. I cringed. Could the weather be any worse?

Staying home today would be far more preferable. I could plunder Father's bookshelves the day long, enjoy endless creamy cups of tea, and dream about the Assembly Ball happening this Saturday and, not long after, Christmas. Excitement welled up. The holidays couldn't come soon enough. I allowed myself a dreamy thought. Would they include romance?

Susan Richard's brothers would be visiting—mayhap this time, I would catch one of the gentleman's interest. She had long plotted my romantic demise with one of them. Would it be Ransom or Luke? They'd been abroad the past few years after completing their education and miraculously remained unattached. Would they recognize me? I was no longer the skin-and-bones girl who tagged after their sister and giggled over much when we tried to spy upon them.

I grimaced at my own reflection—at the dark shadows beneath my eyes. I wouldn't catch anyone's regard looking like that. Not that I believed the thing was entirely dependent on my ability to attract.

The Seasons in Bath were decent, and while I thought I made a fairly amiable dance partner, I'd never made a match past a few well-meaning calls. A bundle of posies, a stiff bow, and the gentlemen would exit my parlor, never returning to further my acquaintance.

Father had jokingly suggested my taking a Season in London. London—where surely the pickings were plentiful among the ton. Mother all but promised I'd be wed within two years. Two years ago. I tossed the old hope aside and gathered my reticule and scarf.

Best not to think about disappointments. Little good it did. Today, Mother and I were to shop for gloves, stop for tea at Lady Ridgeport's house, then stop for tea again at Mrs. Gentry's. Both of whom would while away the calling hours by regaling us with tales of their youth.

This consisted of very old gossip, new gossip, outdated ways of life they preferred, and dishes their former cooks used to make.

Mother had an affinity for the elderly gentlewomen whose husbands had departed this life. And, an affinity for some of that gossip, fresh from their lady's maids. While she didn't approve of gossip in general, she did relish hearing tidbits concerning our acquaintances. Like morsels of cake, information would be doled out for consumption.

Then, she'd do something quite contrary to most who wagged their tongues without regard. She'd pray. Then find a way to be encouraging to the poor soul whose name had been kicked about in the tea parlors. Such was her game. Life was too hard, she'd say, to allow meanness an upper hand.

"Cassandra!" Mother's urgent voice called again as the clock in the hall chimed nine times.

I cast a parting glance at my emptied tea cup, my warm bed, and unfinished needlework by the chair. "Coming—"

Mother flung open my door. "Cassandra!"

I startled away from the mirror and turned. "Forgive me, I did not mean to dilly-dally." I gestured to the window. "Have you seen the weather?"

Mother huffed out of breath, her cheeks flushing apple-pink. She was only half ready for our outing. Her day cap hid a mass of brown and grey frizz, except an uncurled portion had cascaded down her neck. "We aren't to go calling today."

Concern volleyed with uncertainty. "Are you ill? What can I do?"

She waved two messages in the air. "We are disinvited." Her lip curled in disgust. "As though our presence could sully the very teacups we held." She crumpled the notes and tossed them onto the remains of my breakfast tray. "Makes me sick at heart, dear." She pressed the place as though a thorn pierced.

Lady Ridgeport and Mrs. Gentry rarely canceled. "I don't understand. What has happened?" Mother never behaved in such a manner—crumpling invitations? Never. She was decorum itself. At all times.

She shut her eyes, took a stabilizing breath, and spoke again. "We must be brave now, darling." She patted my cheek. "Very brave."

Confusion swirled. "What does bravery have to do with glove shopping and calling?"

"Everything." She licked her lips, pausing for a moment. "We, my dear, are ruined."

Ruined. The word seemed wrong, out of place. Perhaps Mother was ill after all?

Her brows lifted as though still absorbing the fact. "I can see you think me out of my mind, but no, dear. I'm quite sane. We," she huffed another breath to say the word again. "are truly ruined." The terrible truth begged for an explanation.

How does an upstanding family like ours become ruined? Impossible. I couldn't believe it. Wouldn't. There must be some mistake. I made for the door. "I must talk to Father."

Mother snatched my hand and shook her head. "Don't go downstairs, dear. Stay here. I'll have fresh tea sent up."

Doors opening and closing sounded from downstairs. Men's voices echoed.

"What is going on?" My heart beat in quick time. "Why can I not go to him?"

Mother eased down upon my bed. "I'm sure he will tell us about it soon." She tugged the bell pull within reach. "He only told me the most important part." She looked down at her empty hands and then back at me. "That we've lost everything." Her eyes glazed over as she crossed her arms around her middle. "And word of our demise has spread amongst our friends already." Humiliation trembled at her chin.

How could it be so when we'd only just found out? I tossed my reticule to the vanity. Men of business could gossip worse than women, betimes. To tell a wife was to tell the ton. I could hear Lady Ridgeport's pinched voice slicing into the gossip, serving it many times over, her eyes merry with imparting information to the interested parties. *The Chilton's are ruined—utterly ruined!* Horrible woman. Why had we kept connections with her?

The chintz fabric that adorned my bed, the cheerful candlelight, and the bright red knits tossed about seemed to mock the moment. I'd hoped to stay in today and not go visiting. But not like this.

The maid that responded to the bell opened my door. "Lila? Will you take Mother to her room?"

Mother resisted. "No, no. I can't take care of myself." She shooed Lila away. "Just bring us each a tea tray, that's a good girl."

Lila curtsied and left to do as bid. I stood in one place, stunned. "What can I do?"

Mother rose to her feet and huffed. "Nothing. There is nothing to be done." She shuffled to my doorway with slumped shoulders. "Do stay above stairs, Cassandra. Your father is meeting with some important people."

Ruined? Lost... everything?

Just how much of everything?

After a few hours later of pacing and nail-biting, I dared to sneak down the steps and listen to the nearby study door. Seemed Father's solicitor, Mr. Smith, was in attendance—all the way from a village near Birmingham. Were things so dire?

A name was repeated many times. A certain Lord Bandbury and a scandal. What did my good father have to do with such rogues? It wasn't like him. Not at all. Mr. Smith's voice rang loud, "Unfortunate that Banbury's misfortune also be yours. A noose around your neck, man. He may be dead but his greedy claws rise up from the grave, they do, and pull the rope tight-tight-tight!"

I gasped and clapped a hand around my mouth. Such a horrible thing to say!

Father didn't respond. But another gentleman spoke as though to a child. "One ought to be more careful, mind you."

I shrank back from his words. Father was always careful. Intrigues were the stuff of novels and newspapers. Nothing to do with the Chilton family.

I scampered back to my bedroom with a sick feeling in my empty stomach. One thing I knew for certain was that life was about to change, but I couldn't fathom in what ways. Would we be mere subjects of gossip? Or utterly destitute? What would we do? Where would we go?

I changed from my calling dress to an older, more comfortable house dress and slipped down the hall to check on Mother. She sat by the window, watching the icy rain dash upon the bricked streets.

"Sit with me, dear." She motioned to Father's chair that sat opposite hers. "And together, we will plot our course."

"Should we not wait for Father?" Perhaps all was not as lost as she'd said. Maybe she'd heard him wrong. Was quite possible. I wanted to believe it.

She patted her eyes with a handkerchief. "We can dream at least."

Dreams, I knew, were usually the results of good fortunes. Not lost ones. I humored her anyway. I'd do anything to keep worry at bay.

By the end of the afternoon, Mother had envisioned us as pirates who sailed to the Americas and settled in the new frontier. North Carolina, she'd said. Father could be a clerk at some rustic trading post, and she and I would sew muslin gowns for the ladies. Did American ladies appreciate fine muslin?

We began to giggle at the thought when Father's firm footsteps came through the door. His face was pale and sallow. A hand clutched at his heart.

"Excuse us, my dear." His voice was hoarse and weary.

I stood and reached for him. "Father? Should I send for the doctor?"

"No—no." He didn't look at me, only at Mother, with the saddest eyes.

I stepped from the room, closed the door softly, and overheard Father's voice rumble behind me. "We won't be able to live here anymore…"

Our fine house? No longer ours? My stomach squeezed. The worst was true then. Mother and I had surmised as much. What would happen to us?

The tea tray was collected, and a supper tray was brought up. I wasn't sure I could eat. I stepped to the window and watched the busy street below. Carriages rushed by. Neighbors returned from calling, no doubt eager to be out of the foul weather. Rain changed to snow as Mother's sobs drifted down the hall. Her attempt at courage had crumbled.

I'd read many novels of fortunes reversed. Rags to riches, riches to rags. Never did I think it would happen in real life. And what did I really know of real living beyond tea in the parlor and assemblies?

The successful Season in Bath was doomed. London would certainly be out of the picture now.

I chewed my fingernail, which I never did. Nerves beset me. I supposed the best I could hope for was a position as governess. With no siblings of my own, this might be a job I'd enjoy. The last thing I wanted to be was a burden to my parents. If we were in financial straits, there wasn't another option for me.

At school, I'd laughed that I would never have the chance to use French or mathematics. How wrong I was!

The snow thickened, and my stomach growled, despite my protest to not eat. How wrong I've been about many things.

I'd taken everything for granted. I removed the lid from the bowl of creamy soup and took a seat at my lonely table. I lifted the spoon to my lips and thanked God. What else to do in such a moment? We were sustained on this day. Food still lay upon my table. And, for the first time in my life, I thought about something else besides the next Assembly dance.

Ironic how vain it seemed in contrast to our losses—and what I must do, and how that might be offering good to the world in some small way. Strange that I would only think of doing good after losing...everything...this made me feel the fool. Why didn't I believe I could do good before now?

Question after question presented. Would my friends still call me a friend? Did friendship require a percentage of pound notes between us? How did one value friendships outside of the social sphere, who were very much dedicated to themselves? If I did show up at the Assembly on Saturday, would I suddenly become a wallflower? Would I be snubbed? Certainly, no eligible bachelor would come near me. Not now.

But that didn't seem to matter—not in light of my parent's grief. My uncle, the vicar, would tell me to ask God for direction. How long had I been in the habit of merely reciting the Lord's prayer and not using other words?

For a time, it seemed that the words therein were enough. Mayhap they were. A singular phrase stood out and tumbled from my lips, "Your will be done..."

By the time I crawled into bed, Bath was covered in thick, white snow. The streets were abandoned as though time had stopped.

Chapter Two

A week had passed since our predicament presented itself. The mail basket remained depressingly empty of invitations to tea and such, though it seemed I had not lost my dearest friend.

Susan Richards convinced me to still attend the assembly. Perched on the edge of our red damask settee, her pale blonde hair and angelic skin made a striking contrast. She chided me: "My dearest friend, this isn't the time to sit back, no! Quite the opposite. You must employ your charms without delay. Secure a husband before all of Bath knows of your predicament."

"Isn't that rather deceptive?" I shrank from the gossip that had already meandered its way through the ears of the town. Or the truth—whatever form that took. We had well and truly lost the fortune that kept us comfortable.

Susan sipped her tea and pursed her lips. "Every gentleman declares he marries for love and not the dowry. No, my dear. You shall merely beat them at their own game."

"Yes. I see what you mean." I lifted the tea to my lips. Something must be done, or tea would soon be a luxury rather than an expectation. Mayhap, I would work harder to catch a gentleman's eye on Saturday. But again, that didn't seem quite the thing to do.

"You mustn't appear desperate, however. Never that." Susan gazed at me with compassion. "You are an absolute jewel. Don't let anyone let you think otherwise."

"What of your brothers? What will they think of me? A jewel—or?"

Her cup paused at her lips, then clattered to the saucer. "You know I can only speak for myself, Cassandra. I would have you be courted by Ransom, to be sure I would! He is handsome, good, and kind. He will make an excellent husband. But..."

"But?" I already knew the answer.

Her voice dropped low with shame. "Mother has warned him against an attachment to you—as well as Luke."

As would nearly every mother of consequence from here to London. No dowry, no engagement.

Susan set her cup on the tea table and knelt down before me. "Forget what I said about beating a man at his own game." She squeezed her eyes shut. "I wanted to give you hope." She took my hands in hers. "I don't know of any family who would join with yours at this point. But Cassandra, not all men can be so shallow! Surely, there is someone among gentlemen who is truly a gentleman. That love out from their hearts and not because of greed." She blinked back a tear.

"Does such a man exist?" I plucked at a loose string around my sleeve.

She shook her head. "The world is a sad place if they do not." We stood. "I would love nothing better than to have you as a sister."

So. Her parents *had* promptly removed me from the list of possibilities. I had expected it. Furthermore, I expected my advertisement for governess to be far more successful than a swift marriage proposal.

No, indeed. I would not win the heart and hand of any man after one evening of dancing.

"Do say you'll still come with me?" Susan pressed for an answer. "If you are to away soon, we may never have another chance to create a memory together again."

My throat clogged. My life was about to drastically change. I should attend, despite the warnings that would twitter about the room from mothers to sons. Could I withstand the embarrassment? As things stood, I'd never return. "Alright. One last time." For her sake. We had known each other most of our lives, after all.

Susan spun like a child. "I have just the gown for you to borrow. You'll look ravishing."

When I explained to Mother my intention, she gave one of her assenting side nods. I knew she preferred that I stay away from Bath's judgmental eyes. She broke the crust of her pork pie but didn't eat it.

"Do eat. You need your strength, Mother."

She sighed and nibbled a small forkful.

She'd had but one friend to visit and console her. As had I. I suspected the vicar to call shortly. He was fond of my parents.

Otherwise, one wouldn't know we'd spent the whole of our lives in Bath. On this street, in this house...

Father hadn't left his study for hours, so I was surprised when he popped into the dining room with a smile on his face. "Good news, my dear. This is sure to lift your spirits! I know it has mine. Hope is not lost after all."

Mother looked up with interest. Had our fortunes reversed?

"We have been especially invited to be secretary and companion to Lord and Lady Weatherington. They have heard of our circumstances and wish to extend the hand of friendship in this difficult time."

Mother sat, blinking, a blush of pink rising to her cheeks.

"Did you hear me, love? We shall live among our dear friends! Is that not a boon to our situation?"

Lord and Lady Weatherington were good people. Of the best kind, but that glimmer of hope I'd felt slipped down like a sinking sun. My parents would be in service, of sorts.

Mother blinked back tears with a gently sloping smile on her face. "But what of our dearest Cassandra?" She took my hand and grasped it tight.

Father continued. "Naught but twenty miles away, she is expected to serve as governess for the Seal family."

My heart fluttered at the knowledge. The Seals? Had I ever heard of them? I thought not.

Father clapped his palms. "At Lady Weatherington's particular influence. The letter says that nothing but a true lady would be able to teach the Seal girls." Father looked at me with pride. "What say you? I do think the Seals a decent family or Lady Weatherington would never have mentioned you to them."

It was my turn to break the crust of my pork pie but not eat. "I'm sure you are quite right, Father." I attempted a smile. I would teach children, after all. But nothing would ever be the same again.

Mother stood and scanned the missive regarding our occupations. "I rather hoped for more than a governess position for our Cassandra."

Father bowed his head with shame. "I understand. But it cannot be helped. How will you ever forgive me?"

I went to him and wrapped my arms around him. "It wasn't your fault. I'm sure of it."

"If only that were true." His smile wilted. "Enjoy your last dance, Cassandra. I pray it is memorable." He left us to the remains of our supper.

I'd heard that governesses little enjoyed society. While still considered above stairs, a governess was to be as a shadow. Quiet, refined, and disengaged within the drawing rooms and dining halls among the other ladies and gentlemen. She must be present in those situations when their charges must be. Or when at the compassion and mercy of her employer, inclusion would be a condescension.

Worse still, she was never accepted below stairs entirely due to her higher social status. It seemed a lonely occupation. Would I be able to bear the solitude?

But that couldn't be true of every situation. There were good people everywhere. At least, I hoped. And, of course, there were the young ladies to teach. I might make good friends with them and be satisfied with my lot. Susan would be disappointed. I wouldn't make a sudden match as she desired for me. I was no fool to think my life a fairy tale.

One question took precedence. "When do we depart?"

Mother took a deep breath. "In but two weeks, my love. Two weeks."

We wouldn't be together at Christmas. Did she realize it? I couldn't say the words aloud. We'd never been apart for the holiday. Beggars could not be choosers…

For all of my bravado, I couldn't bear the thought of leaving this charming room, this dear dining table, and my parents. Everything and every room suddenly seemed of inestimable value. Never did I think to be without these parts of my life I'd taken for granted. I swallowed forkfuls of the pie without tasting and slipped into my room.

I was to make a lasting memory of the final Assembly I'd ever attend and then leave this place and my family—for good. I must do my part and consider how my situation must engender bravery. Mother's and my grandiose daydreaming of North Carolina had been one thing, the reality quite another.

A package arrived bearing my name. I opened it. The dress—Susan had sent it. I held it against my form. A deep maroon silk shot with green silk ribbon along the hem. Must have cost a fortune. I'd never seen her wear it, not once. An extravagant gift, to be sure!

I lowered the gown. We were of nearly the same size. Had she sacrificed her gown for me? Susan…what would I do without her close by? Letters would have to suffice. I touched the delicate lace along the neckline. I could hardly refuse the gift.

Five short days later, I donned the gown and alighted Susan's family carriage. When Susan made the introductions to Ransom and Luke, they were polite enough, but only just. Ransom coldly handed me into the carriage. I was hardly acknowledged except for Susan, who jabbed them with her icy glances and attempted to rope them into our conversation. They were adept at ignoring her. Indeed.

Ransom was terribly handsome—but would I want his hand if I came with the dowry the ton desired? I was not to be considered, and it was obvious from the start. I gave a laugh, quite unexpectedly. Susan's brothers wouldn't even try to know me, my character, or my heart. Our family's acquaintance was nothing. But I felt a strange peace after seeing what kind of men they really were—these gentlemen that I'd foolishly dreamt about!

I felt sorry for the match they would make in the end. A woman's worth can't be in her father's bank account. Mustn't be! If we hadn't lost everything, might I have been swept away by Ransom's good looks? Or Luke's? Would marriage have been the result and I none the wiser for his reasons? Would they even have admired me—for myself? My character?

Ransom begrudgingly ushered me into my final Assembly and promptly left my side. And, in a matter of minutes, Susan had been whisked away by gentlemen begging for a dance.

Luke, rather embarrassed to be left standing alone with me, asked me to dance but once. He escorted me from the dance floor, bowed, and made some pretense to get me some punch. He never returned. Was I so disagreeable?

Naught else aside from an older gentleman who stepped upon his own foot and regrettably limped back to the chairs from whence he came. I felt sorry for him and to my shame, stifled a laugh. Not because he'd been hurt but because my appeal had been reduced to the sites of a widower in his dotage.

I spotted Lady Ridgeport, who condescended to a mere nod in my direction with no accompanying smile to greet one who had enjoyed countless cups of tea in her parlor.

Not exactly the cut-direct. But a cut nonetheless. Mother would be mortified to know it.

What next? My hand no longer had value. Therefore, I must accept a lack of partners. I took a breath and bid myself to enjoy the music as best as I could. The dancers were quite good, and spirits were high tonight. I'd watch Susan and wait for her to go with me to the supper table.

But it was not to be. Dance after dance, my friend was compromised and I confess, I quite gave up. I turned to go to supper alone when Mr. James, the Master of Ceremonies, bowed before me.

His peppered mutton chop whiskers curved with a smile. "Hm, hm." He bowed again. "Miss Chilton? May I introduce Colonel Nathan Stewart?" He smiled. "Colonel Stewart, Miss Cassandra Chilton."

The colonel bowed. "A pleasure."

I curtsied. His tall form rose above me, his build muscular, his glance as sharp as a bayonet. I wasn't so sure it was a pleasure for him to be introduced to me. Like Susan's brothers.

Mr. James chided him playfully. "Found this bloke standing alone in the corner. Won't do, I said, to see such a fine man and a fine young woman not dancing! And here we are!" His gaze shifted from poor Colonel Stewart to me.

Colonel Stewart cleared his throat. "Would you do me the honor of dancing with me, Miss Chilton?" His sharp gaze had dulled ever so little.

"I thank you, yes." I could not embarrass my host.

The music began. Colonel Stewart took my hand and led me to the floor.

I had to apologize in some way. "I believe you've been coerced into gaining a partner you did not desire." I might as well be plain.

He seemed taken aback. "Coerced is rather a strong word, don't you think?"

"Perhaps. I apologize. I do thank you for taking pity on my singular state along with Mr. James."

His straight lips quirked. "I wouldn't say I asked you to dance entirely out of pity."

I was a charity case, and everyone knew it. And if he didn't know, the ladies within this hall, this very night, would set him straight. Just in case he had romantic notions. Which he didn't, of course not. We were acquaintances of mere minutes.

We danced, and I dared not look him in the eyes again. I might read the truth there. He was being too kind, and I was to be pitied. I saw it in nearly everyone's look when I was greeted upon arrival. I'd even heard a few whispers. This was to be expected. Mother warned me that gossip about our family was still fresh and would be bandied about the room.

Indeed, this Assembly would hold a memory—not of the best. Once one has been reduced before society, well, is there ever a recovery? Mayhap if I had a rich Uncle that died and—but that fairytale thought wasn't feasible. I couldn't think of the flighty what-ifs.

Was all I could do to dance with any sort of enthusiasm. My fine gown notwithstanding, it was clear that I now fit into a different sphere that didn't include assemblies. I might as well accept it.

I would dine, thank Susan, and walk home without telling anyone. I couldn't very well importune Ransom or Luke. I knew my way about Bath and did not fear the night. The cool air would revive me and refresh my thoughts about what must come next.

Yet I was taken by the ease of the colonel's movements. He caught my eye and smiled. His hold, strong but ever so gentle. I couldn't help but enjoy the movements. This was the last time. My last dance, graced with such an amiable gentleman. We moved with the music and I let myself smile too.

The song ended, and Colonel Stewart bowed. I curtsied. He held out his arm to lead me away from the dance floor—but he turned and led me to supper instead. Susan caught my eye, her expression telling.

My silly, romantic friend. She had high hopes.

Colonel Stewart seated me and pulled his own chair. We were served, and those to the left were no acquaintances of mine. We had not been introduced. My only dinner companion was this handsome stranger who'd been compelled to dance with me. I must make the best of it and then—the cold walk home. I accepted that this part of my life was now completely over. I would not be rude, however. I must engage in conversation.

"Colonel, have you been in Bath long?"

"Not long, not above three days."

I noted a faint pink scar along his neck—where his cravat did not cover. "And will you take a house here?"

He shook his head. "If only I could, though I may be tempted to rent rooms upon summer."

"Do you enjoy the sea?" His uniform was that of infantry—not of the navy. Was more of a horseman, I daresay.

"Immensely." He smiled—and those eyes that I had first thought sharp took on a new hue. A deep golden brown that warmed with a dream. "But I must away to my estate—and other responsibilities."

"As must I."

"You've an estate?"

Color rushed to my cheeks. "Not at all. Responsibilities, I mean. I, too, must leave this wonderful seaside and grapple with my duty."

"Then we are of one purpose." He lifted his wine glass. "Let us toast." He smiled. "To fulfill our duties."

I lifted my glass with his and drank. I don't quite know why, but we began to laugh. I suddenly felt free of pretension. We, both of us, singularly needed to go about as life would have us—recognizing that in each other.

"The seaside is—how can I describe it? An ever-flowing force that one can always count upon, but different every single day."

"Do you swim?" He asked with a lifted brow.

I smiled in return. "I don't even need the bathing machine." I looked at my plate of ham and stewed fruits. Had I known last summer that my dips in the ocean would likely be my last, I might have relished them all the more.

He nodded. "Well done. I approve. I believe every woman ought to know how to swim."

"And man, I hope."

His eyes crinkled with humor. "But of course. Yes." He laughed. "Men, too."

I finished my plate with much better spirits than I began it. Was as though I'd made a friend of this handsome colonel, if only for an hour.

He pulled my chair again when we'd finished. "You are no doubt anxious to return to the dance floor." He bowed again. "I am away early, so I beg you good night."

I curtsied, "Good night, Colonel Stewart."

His brown eyes stayed upon mine for the merest second, and my heart gave a small flip. I thought he might say something—but no words came.

So, this is what it's like to meet a fine prospect...

I closed my eyes briefly against the impossibility as his back retreated to the cloakroom and through the front double doors. I would never see him again. At least I'd not been so alone for the last hour. A kind companion had been provided. I could thank God for this and move on as I intended.

I waited a moment then made my way to the cloakroom too. The maid tightened the wool cape around my shoulders, and I tugged on my gloves and bonnet. I quite left the premises without informing Susan. A few steps into my walk, I heard a voice behind me.

"Surely you do not walk alone? At night?"

My heart leaped as I turned toward the steps of the Assembly Hall. Colonel Stewart. He hadn't left yet. I glanced at the moon shining brightly behind his shoulder. I couldn't look into his eyes. Not again. "I find that cold air helps clear the mind."

"You do not fear the night—or those that prefer it?"

I swallowed. Since he put it that way... I wasn't sure. "I confess that while I've walked these streets the whole of my life, I hadn't given my safety consideration."

"What of your escort?"

I shook my head. "The Richards are well occupied. I didn't want to disturb them. Perhaps I should go back inside and wait until they are ready to depart."

He held out his arm. "I find, Miss Chilton, that cold air helps clear my mind as well. It would be my pleasure to see you safely home."

"You are too kind." I slipped my hand into his waiting arm and gave direction.

Chapter Three

Patches of snow still gathered about the shadowed corners of the townhouses and buildings along the street. Puddles caught the moon gleams, and where they didn't, they had turned into slick black ice.

I lost my balance, slipping without any decorum, like a clumsy dance partner pulling on his arm.

Colonel Stewart acted quickly, gripping me tight and pulling me up. "Not even a sensible thief would traverse such dangerous paths."

His voice held edges of stern, concern, and a jest all at once.

"Then it is a good thing I'm not a sensible thief."

"Watch out, there's another." He pulled me closer as we walked around the offending ice.

"I daresay I don't know what I would do without your kind offer to see me home." I cleared my throat. "I might have broken an ankle or worse."

"Mmm. I should have called a carriage, indeed." He murmured. "I confess to being quite taken by your desire to be out in the cold for a brisk walk."

I dashed my eyes up to the clear, bright stars. Did they shine as clearly where I was going? "And here we are, fighting the evils of knowing we must leave Bath for different pastures—and—nature's warning that we ought to have stayed off her walkways and inside the safety of our warm kitchens until she withdraws."

Colonel Stewart asked, "Is leaving Bath an evil thing for you? I sense you do not want it."

Leaving wasn't evil, no, but the reasons for my needing to leave? I wasn't so sure. Father didn't entirely explain how his fortune had been siphoned away by someone named Banbury. Only that it had, and we must retrench down to the pence. I needed to answer Colonel Stewart but hesitated.

"You are reluctant—do forgive me, Miss Chilton. I do not wish to pry. Your circumstances are your own, and I do respect them."

"It is alright—I daresay if you haven't heard rumors about my family by morning, you most certainly will by afternoon."

"Oh?"

He hadn't heard, and for some strange reason, my heart sank. I'd hoped he already knew and still desired to be a friend, though I might argue that it was still pity that propelled him to his gentlemanly ways...

"I'm to be a governess."

"Ah."

"How old are your charges?"

"I don't yet know."

"Do you desire this work?"

"I've no choice in the matter as I must learn to support myself. I do rather enjoy the thought of being of some good to young ones. I'll be honest," I had nothing to lose by speaking my heart. I'd never see him again after tonight. "I find that I've been far too idle. I've been wondering how my days, including taking tea and listening to women gossip, have possibly done me any benefit—or anyone else. I find that I am glad to discover my life must consist of doing something worthwhile. Or worthy of God, at the very least." I gulped at his silence. I'd said too much. "While you, Colonel, have been—where?"

His voice took on a quiet tone as he finished my sentence. "In the Peninsula, fighting Napoleon's invasion."

I'd seen a line of scarring. From the war? Likely. I cringed at what he must have endured. War was terrible.

I resumed my query. "Now that you've returned, you must see to your estate?"

"Mm, yes. It has been too long neglected. My older brother died two years ago, and the workings have been in the hands of my steward since. High time I beat my sword to the plowshare if you will."

"I quite understand. Will your homecoming be a joyous occasion?"

He slowed his steps. "A quiet one, more like. I've no family left aside from a sister who lives in Plymouth. She is much occupied with her children and husband."

"I always desired a sister. Or a brother. It has only been my parents and me the whole of my life. Indeed, all is about to change."

Home was but three houses down. In mere steps, my acquaintance with this gentleman would end. "We are nearly there. See? It's the one where two lanterns are lit by the red door." I suddenly thought of the impropriety of our situation. Neither of us had thought about the consequences of walking together alone at night.

I believed us both entirely swept away by our circumstances—and he being a gentleman—cared enough to be my protector for a short walk. Wasn't as though any old gossip thought to peer through her curtains and spy upon us. Was nearing midnight, after all. No—no harm done. I was sure of it.

He led me up my steps, thankfully swept clean of snow and ice. He was bowing over my hand when the door swung open.

Father. "Cassandra! What is the meaning of this? Where, indeed, are the Richards?" His jaw slackened at the unexpected scene.

Colonel Stewart stepped back, eyes wide, form erect.

"Father, do not be concerned. All is well. The Richards are likely to be occupied for a few more hours—and I—" excuses fell splat even as I tried to create a plausible reason to offer.

Colonel Stewart bowed. "Sir—Mr. Chilton. Forgive my boldness and the late hour. I noted Miss Chilton in need of assistance as it appeared her escort was truly occupied, and the ice along the route was rather precarious. Otherwise, I would never have presumed."

"Ice, eh?" His expression dropped. "And the Richards brothers did not see fit to look after you? The brothers of your dearest friend? Tis shameful."

The concept of duty and honor was complicated for gentlemen seeking to further their fortunes through marriage. Twas certainly ungentlemanly of them. But thinking of Susan—too occupied to even sup with me stung. Her conquests were many tonight.

Father moved so we could enter. "Well, nothing for it, but do come in and warm yourself before you return to wherever it is you're staying."

We entered the foyer, and I turned to Colonel Stewart and curtsied. "I thank you for your assistance and pray you good fortune in your endeavors."

He bowed. "It has been a pleasure, Miss Chilton.

This was it then. The true farewell. I climbed the steps, mindful of my father's offer to him for a cup of tea by the fire in his study. Would that the world was full of men as kind as Colonel Stewart...

Lila helped me ready for bed. I thanked her profusely for the hot bricks she'd slipped beneath the blankets. My feet had quite gone numb with the cold on the walk home. But the rest of me—oh, the rest of me would never forget this night. Only it wouldn't be time with Susan that I remembered with great fondness.

Was an interesting thing how the kindness of one man so affected me! Well then.

Lila snuffed out the candle and left me to my own thoughts. If I were to fall in love with anyone, I'd want him to be like Colonel Stewart.

Was safe to think it, to dream it even. A lovely standard I would both aspire to and wait for. Though I would likely spend my younger days employed and out of the sight of the likes of such men, I would think of our time together and remember. And cherish the memory.

I rolled over and blinked away a tear of grief. Dreams were wily things. Volatile and unreliable wonderings. Oh, but I liked Colonel Stewart.

A few minutes later, I heard the front door open and close. I imagined him retracing our steps until the back of him disappeared. I would never see him again.

I took a final deep breath and allowed sleep to take me.

Chapter Four

Mother had an unusually bright countenance in the morning. She even hummed a tune between bites of toast. After these last few days of strain, twas a relief to see a modicum of joy about her. She continued to cast loving glances my way until she finally spoke.

"What if, my dear, there was quite another course of action for you?"

"Yes, Mother?" I scooped egg from the cup and plopped a bit onto my toast. "You mean instead of governess? Can't imagine what you have in mind." I hadn't the ability to go into any sort of trade. I'd never actually sewn my own gowns. However, I had been taught to hem and stitch the finer things. Embroider cushions and the like. "I might rather work with children, truly."

"Yes..." her voice trailed off, and I wondered what she was thinking. It would be impertinent to ask. A dim smile lit her lips as she spread jam on her bread.

Poor Mother. She'd been thinking about my plight a great deal. "Tis a shame you can't work at Lord and Lady

Weatherington with us! But as Lady Weatherington stated, she refuses to place you in a position below your status."

Below my status…I wondered if my status was something to consider. I suppose I was of the more useless sort. Born and bred a lady but suitable for little outside of replenishing the next generation of ladies with things ladies ought to know. My situation was laughable!

Had I been a farmer's daughter, down on her luck, I'd be able to milk cows, make cheese, and who knows what else. Indeed, I felt quite out of any useful sphere. I wasn't even marriageable because of my status. Who would desire the dreaded governess?

Lila arrived with a smile on her lips as she handed forth a bouquet—a clutch of crimson and white roses—a lavish expense considering the time of year.

The message caused my heart to stop.

Dear Miss Chilton,

I thank you for the honor of your acquaintance, the pleasurable dance, supper, and walk. My mind is quite clear with steadfast purpose. I owe it to you for suggesting such exercise. Do not forget to take a shell from the beach with you so that you might still hear the ocean and remember its endless possibilities.

Safe travels,

Col. Nate Stewart

I wanted to bury my face in the beauty of those blossoms if only to hide the blush that rose to my face.

A few days passed of packing away personal belongings, sorting through items I might find useful in my new position, and the horrifying ordeal of watching strangers tour our home that they might find it suitable to rent.

The house took on a rather foreign appearance, what with family portraits taken down and some furnishings sold. I slogged through the days, putting on a brave front but weeping at night. The future swiftly became a reality.

I'd not known life without my family. Time ticked, and we were brief moments away from spending the rest of our lives apart. As it were, my dear Mama and Papa called me to them during tea. My favorite tarts were upon the platter, along with delectable olives and the like. Were we to have a party?

Mother poured tea. "Do you recall my thoughts the other morning, Cassandra?"

I nodded. "Yes." They were as yet unfinished and unexplained.

"Well." She handed me a hot cuppa. "It has come to your Father's and my attention that there truly might be another path for you to take aside from being a governess."

Another path? Unlikely. "But it's all settled, isn't it? In your reply to Lady Weatherington and Mrs. Seals?"

Father took a tart from the plate. "Not entirely." He bit into the thick lemon filling.

"I don't understand."

Father finished his tart and dusted his fingers of the crumbs. "You were never meant to suffer, dearest. I made a terrible mistake, and I won't stand by and see you endure the worst of it. No, indeed, I won't!"

Mother's lips pursed. "What your father means to say is that we—you—you've been offered a more permanent situation." She allowed her statement to sink in.

"Permanent?" Even as I repeated the word, I knew what would come after.

Father smiled. "Marriage, my dear. Security!" He leaned forward. "Cassandra, the gentleman who offers for you has not only an upstanding reputation but a true desire to see you well-set."

"What your father means to say—" Mother shot him a glance once again, "is that we've been made an offer for your marriage, and we agree. All that remains is for you to also agree."

The olives and lemon tart sat like a stone in my stomach.

Mother scooted closer to me like old Lady Ridgeport about to share a tidbit of gossip. "The gentleman in question is to raise a pair of young wards. You won't believe it, but I've had a letter from my uncle, the vicar in Butterton. The gentleman in question came to him seeking a potential match and he thought of you instantly! Isn't that Providential?"

Providential? I was stunned. Marriage...to a stranger? Wards. Children.

Father cleared his throat and blinked rapidly. "My girl, I thought you'd be pleased."

I licked my lips and tried to be interested. It was all so sudden. "This man—he needs a mother figure for his wards?"

"Desperately." Mother put a hand on my back and rubbed. "He plans to raise them himself as though belonging to him. I know you were always disappointed not to have siblings. More children about the place would have been a delight. In this way, as a wife, you will retain your status and respect. You will be not only provided for but cared for."

I thought of the roses that hadn't yet withered on my dressing table. "And what if we do not suit?"

"Alas—this has been considered, though from what my Uncle Harris says, he thinks you shall get along admirably. You will travel to Butterton to stay with him and his new wife to spend several days before Christmas. The gentleman and the children will be in attendance for the introduction. If you agree to the match," Mother clapped her hands. "Then you shall be married by Christmas Day. Uncle will officiate himself."

Father placed a hand over his heart. "Think of it, dear—you'd be saving your old father his heavy guilt of making such a gross mistake."

And perhaps loosening the noose that held a chokehold around his neck. "Father—you know I do not blame you."

His brows rose, then fell. "I shall feel much better to see you settled with so honorable a man."

Was honor better than love? Perhaps it was. He was willing to take Great Uncle Harris' word of my character, though I hadn't seen Uncle Harris for nearly a year.

"Our daughter is a romantic, John." Mother heaped a plate full and put it into my hands. "Do eat, and do know that in the end, it's God that puts people together. He is also a romantic, you see. I do believe a better kind of love will grow between you in time."

I mindlessly popped an olive into my mouth.

Father shoved my teacup across the table towards me. "You are to go to Butterton, but the choice is yours. If, after the holiday, you find you cannot abide the man to marry him, well. We shall employ Lady Weatherington's influence for a situation once more."

Twas fair. More than fair. "Alright. I will go to Butterton." I didn't have to marry him if I didn't desire it. I would truly like to see Uncle Harris again and meet his new wife.

I would have to entirely set aside my dreamy thoughts concerning Colonel Stewart. And the roses he'd sent.

"When do I leave?"

Mother and Father looked at each other before Mother spoke. "In but two days, dear." They each took one of my hands. "I despise that we must spend Christmas apart. So, tomorrow, we shall have one last evening just us three together. We shall break out the Christmas pudding early for the occasion."

In two days...time would fly in a blink.

That afternoon, Susan appeared much penitent for her abandonment of me during my final assembly dance.

"Cassandra! I was quite beset with gentlemen! I couldn't turn about without being asked to dance or to take a turn about the room." Her cheeks flushed with color.

"So I noticed." I gave an encouraging smile, for that is what she wished for. My approval so that her guilt might be assuaged.

She lowered her head. "My brothers were indomitably rude—to abandon you as they did."

No one corrected the slight. "It is alright, Susan. I didn't expect my hand to be much desired." However, I had expected some care for my evening as they were the ones who were generous enough to supply me with a gown and a ride.

Lila brought in the tea tray. I poured a cup for Susan and added cream. We'd no more sugar nor coin to purchase such a sudden extravagance. Father mentioned that we mightn't like how sugar was procured if we knew of what the trade entailed. *High time we abandon its use,* he'd muttered under his breath. I handed Susan her cup.

She sipped her tea and winced at the lack of sweetness. "When must you depart?"

"Wednesday morning, I'm told."

Susan set the teacup down and threw her arms around me. "Life simply won't be the same any longer."

No. It certainly wouldn't.

Chapter Five

My carriage arrived with little ceremony. My trunks had been packed to the brim. I'd hugged Lila's neck and Cook's, then my parents. Susan had not returned, stating the farewell was far too painful for her to endure another goodbye. We'd promised to write.

I did not reveal to her my change in plans to meet a stranger and possibly marry him. No need for gossip to snake around Bath's parlors about the doomed Chilton debutante.

Father held back, swallowing and swiping at his eyes with a great handkerchief. Mother guided me down the steps to the carriage, "Best go quickly, daughter, before your father becomes a weeping fool."

I clutched my straw bag as I was handed within—a luxury provided by my would-be fiancé.

The carriage was plush with comfort. Pillows rested in each corner, along with a box of hot coals for my feet and a thick, green plaid blanket. My insides warmed at the thoughtfulness. Whoever this gentleman was, he was kind. Indeed, he'd ordered the best fit for a princess with a significant dowry.

Did he know of our financial state? I would think that my Uncle Harris would have informed him of this terrible fact before sending for me.

I tossed a final wave to Lila, my maid whose tears had been evident the whole morning. I was loathe to lose her ministrations, indeed. But she could not be pressed upon to leave Bath and her family, not for any cost.

I wondered at our differences—my having to do so, but my maid being poor enough and free enough to choose to stay. The carriage lurched forward. I peered one last time through the window, only to see my parents' backs reenter the house. They, too, would travel a few days hence to their new home at the Weatherington estate.

I grew tearful as we passed each building and lane. I was to Butterton. To affiance myself to a man I didn't know, to be a wife and mother to his wards. If I so desired. If...

I'd many, many hours of travel before me, two days of continuous riding at the very least. If only a friend could have come with me. Or Mother and Father... I'd never been quite so alone. Not even a female companion could be afforded. I daresay my would-be suitor had not thought of it.

Was I so... expendable? I gave another glance around this spacious, comfortable carriage. Twas confusing. Ah, well. I would daydream as Mother had taught me to do. Come up with stories, no matter how silly. A fun way to while away the hours—though none to laugh with over the impossible scenarios.

The bleak sky remained dull for the rest of my journey that day. Entirely uneventful, the carriage finally pulled into a coaching inn whose cheery warmth seemed sufficient enough. One of the maids assisted me to my room and delivered my solitary supper of bread and lamb stew. The good young woman stayed with me through the night so that I might not fear the male guests who drank below or the snores I might hear echoing down the hall.

I thanked her profusely as she pulled a trundle be from beneath mine.

"Tis no bother, miss." She grinned with a full set of teeth. "I'm right tired if you don't mind my saying."

I stretched my sore muscles, donned my nightgown, ate my fill, and fell into a dreamless stupor, so exhausted was I.

The next day, the driver and I made off once again for another very long day of naught but passing through much countryside and my dreamy wonderings. A few hours into the journey, rain began to fall. First lightly, then, it fell at such a rate that the carriage was forced to stop entirely.

A knock rattled my door and opened. "Aye, miss, I've to go down the road to see where the closest inn may be." Thunder rattled the air, and the rain blew in sheets. He held his hat tight against the wind. "Didn't count on getting caught in this sludge. Mud's near impassable."

"Oh my. Of course, do as you see fit."

He gave a curt nod. "I'll return for ye directly and see ye safely settled as soon as may be."

I'd be left alone. "Alright." I supposed he had to do what he had to do. No way around it.

"You've naught to fear, miss. No souls dare be out in this weather, mind ye. But if it makes ye feel safe, there's a pistol in the box." He jerked his chin. "Just there."

"I thank you, I'm sure I won't need to touch it."

"Daresay, you won't. Right then, off I go!"

And there I sat. The driver marched away, and I was entirely alone in a strange place for the first time in my life. Thunder rocked the carriage, and I shuddered, gathering my cloak more tightly about my shoulders. A sliver of fear slipped up my spine, or was that a chill? None had filled the coal box to warm my feet this day. The air grew colder with each passing minute.

I shivered and drew the blanket about my legs, waiting, waiting, waiting. I waited ever so long. Thunder seemed like a never-ending giant throwing a tantrum above my head.

How long was I to be alone? Finally, I tossed the blanket aside and checked the box where the weapon was. I unlatched the lid and spied the small silver pistol. Heavens, but it seemed deadly. I snapped the box shut again. It was of little use as I didn't know how to operate it.

Not that I feared being found by a—a smack hit the carriage, and I squealed. Followed by more smacks. Twas hail! Icy stones pummeled in a loud roar. The window cracked and crumbled away from the door. I burrowed to the other side and thought it better to stay in the center.

Was so dark, I wished for a light, even a small one. If only my driver returned with all haste and I could once again snuggle safely in bed. Surely, the journey would be better on the morrow.

As it were, he did not come. For hours, I sat. The hail had stopped long ago. The sun, what little there was by the end of the hail's assault on the world, hardly lent light to the twilight. Had my driver become injured in the storm? Did he lie on the road waiting for help? Mayhap he waited for me?

My heart thumped as the possibility became real. He wouldn't have simply abandoned me once he reached the inn. He promised he'd come back directly. But how could I traverse the dark, icy roads as night fast approached?

My stomach growled. I had not eaten since breakfast, and my flask of tea was empty. I wanted to cry like a child.

If I stayed, I was alone. If I trekked down the road, I'd still be alone. I didn't even have a lantern—wait—I opened the carriage door and gingerly stepped into sludge. The hail had broken the lanterns hanging on either side of the carriage. I'd no way to light them in any case. Even if the driver lay beside the road, I wouldn't be able to spot him without light.

A howl sounded in the distance. I hied to my place and locked the door. Within the hour, full darkness came upon the landscape. I was truly stuck. I allowed one tear to slip down my cheek. I forced myself to be as brave as the heroines in the novels I've read and in the stories I made up in my head.

I shivered and couldn't stop. It was so very cold. I lay stretched out upon the seat, bundled as best as I could. I didn't know it was possible to be so chilled! I lay so for hours as the night deepened and my hope dashed.

At first light, I'd walk the road. Surely someone would help me. I prayed to God for help. For help now—it needn't wait.

Indeed, did ice flow through my veins? I swallowed with a dry throat. If only I had a full flask of tea, I might survive this predicament.

Sometime later, something prodded me. Pushed. I startled awake and screamed and gasped within a blast of freezing air.

"Hold steady, miss. I'm here to help you." A deep, strong voice—so warm—met my ear. "Are you injured?"

"No." My voice shook from the cold as my eyes adjusted to the shadowed face before me.

He lifted me outside, and I blinked. He blinked. We said each other's names in unison, his the louder, mine weak with cold. "Miss Chilton!"

"Colonel Stewart." My lips trembled. Was I dreaming? But no. His tall form, his sandy hair, hatless, his eyes—concerned.

"I beg you to put me down." To be discovered in such a state! I must look a fright.

He cocked a brow. "Are you sure?"

I wasn't. I couldn't feel my feet. My hands were numb with cold.

He slowly placed me upright, and I buckled. He lifted me in his arms once again and looked down at me, worry tinging his voice, "You are ill, I'm afraid."

"I dearly hope not." Illness could impede my potential engagement. I shuddered. The shock of seeing Colonel Stewart again set my thoughts stuttering. This couldn't be happening...

"Mmm." He glanced down the road ahead. We need to find an inn." He set me back into the freezing coach, threw his gloves off, and proceeded to take mine off as well.

"What do you?"

He placed my hands between his and rubbed hard, chaffing heat back into my fingers, if only a little. Slivers of pain prickled. That's when I noticed his torn jacket and a bruise on his jaw. I looked about for a horse— none.

"Any better?" He paused the rubbing and handed me my gloves.

"Some. I thank you." I stretched my fingers before sliding the gloves back on. "Colonel Stewart? How came you to be here?"

He evaded my question with one of his own, his eyes as sharp as when we were first introduced. "Answer me first—where is your driver?"

"He left amid the storms yesterday to find an inn. The coach is stuck, as you see. He didn't make it back. I fear he is harmed." My mind had conjured all manner of possibilities. Surely he hadn't died...

"Or perhaps he stopped for a drink and had too many." He grimaced. "I shouldn't think the worst of the man, but if I find him uninjured, Miss Chilton, there will be a price to pay." He looked around me. "Have you no companion at all?"

My parents had been loathed to send me without one. It wasn't done. But when the fine carriage arrived, it eased their minds. The journey was to last but a few days and no more. "Alas, my maid could not find it within herself to leave Bath behind, so dearly she loves her home."

"Ah. And you are quite alone and cold." He tugged his gloves on again, too. "Dash it all. My horse was stolen last night, or I would have you ride him." His lips quirked. "Once again, I must escort you safely, Miss Chilton. You simply cannot remain in this freezing weather. Indeed, I fear for your health. You must allow me to carry you."

My eyes smarted. He was right, but I was mortified.

"Did you ever ride piggyback as a child?"

I shook my head. "No siblings to frolic so."

"Miss Chilton, I'll have you know that I'm a man of honor. I would not require this of you if there were any other way."

"I understand."

"You will have to hitch your skirts up a bit and ride upon my back. You have seen it done, I hope?"

I nodded. The fisherman's children played it often on the shores of Bath.

"Good."

"What if I am too heavy?"

"You are a feather compared to the men I've carried from the battlefield..." his voice trailed off. "You need a warm fire and food. Sooner, the better." His eyes bore concern with a wrinkle of amusement about them. What we were about to do seemed utterly silly, but there was no help for it. Quite literally.

"Alright."

"Raise your skirts." He turned his back so he couldn't see me. I was thankful. "Now wrap your arms around my chest and grip—I'm a dunce." He whirled about just as I dropped my skirts. He clapped a hand to his eyes. "Forgive your rescuer for his inability to think straight. It has been a long night. I will unlatch one of these horses, and we will ride."

I looked at the giant beast who stamped his hoof into the mud, clearly not amused with the prospect. "We shall have to ride bareback with no reins..."

"You have a point. This may not be possible. Piggyback it is."

My chin trembled. I'd endured a wretched night and had been found by the gentleman I was going to have to forget at all costs. He would be my rescuer, and then he would take his leave once again. Would that my suitor could be so gallant.

"I am sorry, Miss Chilton. You should never have been abandoned so. But since I have a habit of rescuing you in the cold, I shall gladly be your horse. Pig. Whatever you want to call it."

I stifled a laugh and launched upon his back. "Walk on, Colonel Stewart." I still could not believe it was he that found me. I'd not breathed a word about Colonel Stewart to Susan, but I wondered what she would think. Her brothers were nothing compared to the kindness of this man.

I clung to his back for nearly two miles before an inn blessedly came into view. It had been so close! I had no idea. Had I chanced the road last night, I might not be so miserable as in this moment. Exhausted and frozen through. If only my driver had returned.

"Do let me try to walk now. You have warmed me." As soon as the words were out of my mouth, I regretted them. The man did warm me, inside and out. It was a wrong feeling knowing

I was on my way to meet my potential fiancé—and, perhaps, husband.

"As you wish."

He took my arm and tucked me close to his side as he'd done but a week ago. My feet finally had some feeling back into them, but my head ached so! We approached the inn, having caught no sight of my driver lying injured on the road. Was he here?

The question was soon answered as we stepped through the door. The man himself, dressed and rested, hat atop his head. His mouth hung agape, his eyes registering shock.

"Miss!"

Colonel Stewart spoke in a tone likely used upon those ranked below him. "Am I to understand that you were her driver?"

The man dipped his head.

"You ought to be flogged." Colonel Stewart released me and towered over the man.

I spoke up. "Why did you not return for me?" I wanted to be angry, but I was so tired. Far too tired to really care any longer.

Holding his hands against the formidable colonel, the driver stuttered his excuse. "They said you was come, miss, that you were led above stairs. That you'd been dropped off by some kind soul. Or I would have never left you! I swear it!"

Colonel Stewart pushed him aside and led me within. "Did you not think to verify the woman's identity?"

"Didn't think. Weren't no soul out in such as last night—who else could it have been?" His face reddened. "I didn't think. I'm sorry, miss." He adjusted his collar. "I'll be fetching the coach now, miss."

"Wait while I get Miss Chilton settled."

Colonel Stewart led me to the fireplace, the space blessedly empty of patrons, and onto the slender bench before it. He pressed a gentle squeeze to my shoulder. "Wait here."

How was it possible for my body to ache so when I have done naught but shiver and be carried all the way here?

The fire's heat swam before my face, tingling my skin awake. Colonel Stewart and the driver had stepped outside, but, by chance, they positioned just outside the window beside me. I could hear them. Colonel Stewart's voice was strong and carried straight through the thin window glass.

"When I hired you to carry her to Butterton, I was told that you were the best driver available. Not some irresponsible thoughtless—"

"Colonel Stewart, sir, I had no idea twas you—"

A cup of tea was placed in my hands. I trembled yet more. What had he just said? *When I hired you to carry her to Butterton...*

When *I* hired you to carry her to Butterton.

The plush coach ride had been a gift from my potential fiancé. Colonel Stewart? Now every part of me burned. But how? I sipped my hot tea, my eyes shuttering closed, blinking back tears that came regardless of my design to stop them.

From the dance at the assembly, through the days of packing and wondering who the man of mystery was—I'd even tossed his roses at the end so I wouldn't daydream of Colonel Stewart any longer. Wouldn't be fitting! And now, he was here, having rescued me from the coach he'd supplied? After he'd clearly been in a brawl?

I took another swallow and allowed the hot liquid to soothe. Nothing made sense, except for the man that returned to my side with a cup of tea in his hands.

Was he really, truly the gentleman who required a spouse? I dared a glance at him.

"Miss Chilton—feeling better?"

"Colonel Stewart..." I looked down at my tea again. "I...heard you through the window."

His face reddened as he set his cup down. "I beg your patience. I had no intention of sending you on a reckless journey that could have cost you your life. Will you forgive me? For not protecting you enough?" His face was in earnest.

"Perhaps I did not hear correctly." I set my empty teacup into the saucer and clenched my hands in my lap. "You—you are the gentleman whom Uncle Harris...the vicar whom..." I failed to finish my sentence. It was all so inconceivable.

He sat beside me on the bench. "I have a confession to make." A quirk lifted on the side of his lips. "I traveled to Bath expressly to make your acquaintance."

"You—" I trembled all the more. "You are the one..." Wonder and nerves vied for position.

He looked at me with frankness. "I didn't desire to waste my time or yours if we failed to even have an amicable conversation."

We'd been more than amicable. We'd been shy during the dance, but dinner and our walk home had been...wonderful. My face flashed with heat, not of the fire. "You already knew of my circumstances?"

"I am sorry I was not forthcoming on that score. Once we were introduced, I lost my way a bit. Meeting someone for the first time whom one might make significant life changes with rather jumbled my thinking."

"Why me?"

"Why not you?" He laughed softly. "Your vicar uncle spoke highly of you, your genuine nature, your kindness," he paused, "your beauty..."

"You flatter sir."

"I only repeat your uncle's words. You can't imagine how I felt when I found his praises to be true—and more."

I looked away from his warm gaze. He required a wife. Desired one in haste. I was a convenience but...the way he looked at me, I felt as though I was truly living within a romance novel. Had I not felt a difference upon his acquaintance, though short it was? And his bouquet of roses I loathed to leave behind?

How could I feel such strength behind our meeting and now know his purpose? But I did, and it frightened me a little. He planned to take me as his bride if I agreed. Uncle Harris approved of him, but he was yet a stranger.

It resembled a romance, but might I trust it? I looked back at him, and he continued.

"Imagine my surprise when you told me of your desire to do more in this world. To make more of yourself—what was it?

Beyond gossip in the parlors and assemblies? You seemed eager to teach children."

"Indeed. I do. I am..."

He smiled. "How could I resist wanting to know a woman like that?"

"Colonel Stewart, if you don't mind my saying, you would do much better with a London Season. Surely there are young women of great benefit...I..." What was I saying? This was the man I dearly wanted to see again. He didn't seem to mind I came with nothing.

"Great benefit?" His brows rose, and he held up his index finger. "I endured one month, October past to be precise, of that wretched Season." He swiped a hand through his hair. "Never again. I've not seen so many ridiculous females gathered to spear a man with her charms in all my life—tis not worth a dowry of any size."

I blinked at how quickly and easily I'd devalued myself by monetary comparison—the very thing that began to gall me. "Understood."

"Miss Chilton." He reached over and caught my hand in his. "I've been a man of tents and war and battle. I've known death and hunger. I know how one choice can change a life forever. The world can be a hard place." His eyes did not weep, but I thought they might. "And because of that, I've two wards to raise. I refuse to acquire a selfish wife who only cares about society and position with all the trappings." He took my other hand. "I desire a wife who will love my wards as her own children would be loved. They've endured far too much loss for anything less."

My eyes smarted. Had he also endured too much loss? I'd forgotten about the wards. "How old are they?"

"Rachel is but six years old. Her brother, Andrew, is eight."

"All they have is each other?" I swallowed down my emotions.

He shook his head. "They have me and…" He let the question dangle between us. He released my hands. "A question best answered later." He smiled. "You need to rest—I've sent for a doctor and hired a maid to see to your needs. Do you think you can climb the stairs?"

I rose to my feet and wobbled.

"Nonsense. Up we go." He lifted me in his arms, no piggyback this time. My arms had nowhere to go but around his broad shoulder and across his chest.

I was so very, very tired. He lay me on the bed and left me to the maid's ministrations and the doctor's order that I rest a few days in this place before traveling once again. I insisted I was fine but readily knew that Colonel Stewart wasn't a man to be deterred from his purpose.

I was his purpose.

My heart thudded even as my eyelids scarce could stay open. I'd been inclined to accept the gentleman offering, despite him being a stranger. I'd been resigning myself to this good kind of duty. But now that I knew the man was Colonel Stewart—my heart couldn't help but be involved. Might love grow to exist between us?

Chapter Six

A more luxurious rest I've never enjoyed. The maid waited upon me, hand and foot. Which mostly meant several bowls of hot pea soup, pots of tea, and one hot bath ordered by the physician. Colonel Stewart had sent for thick woolen socks and had procured a novel to help pass the time.

All the while, I was outright distracted by our last interaction. I'd not just time to rest, but to think and think—only my imagination quite ran away with me instead and I couldn't quite think so clearly beyond the fact that Colonel Stewart had sought me based upon my great uncle's description and found me pleasing enough to the point of desiring to call me "wife."

Trust and goodness were an entirely different kind of currency in which to exchange—one vow with another...

The carriage had arrived along with my trunks which thankfully had not been stolen. But, I began to wonder of Colonel Stewart's own horse—and his appearance when he came to my aid. He'd been in a brawl? Or had he the misfortune of being caught in the hail storm?

What exactly had happened? I'd been in too exhausted a stupor to give that fact a thought until now. I'd been lost in my dreams. Of marriage and the choice I must make.

I drew my laundered cloak about my shoulders as the maid adjusted my bonnet. Was time to travel. I was fully rested and healed from that terrible cold night. And Colonel Stewart waited below stairs.

Next, we would travel to my uncle's home for Christmas, where, Colonel Stewart said the children waited for us.

I was eager to be there now. To see family and meet Andrew and Rachel. To celebrate the holiday and the possible new beginning. I went downstairs where he stood tall at the newel post.

"Miss Chilton." He bowed and offered me his hand. "We've many hours before us. Are you certain you are up for the trip?"

"I can bear it if you can." Travel wasn't the most comfortable of occupations.

He smiled. "Indeed."

We alighted the carriage together this time, albeit with a new driver. Colonel Stewart insisted on being my protector all the way to Butterton—regardless of no companion or chaperone between us. Twould be a scandal if those of my acquaintance in Bath knew of it. But I trusted Colonel Stewart—as did my uncle. What had I to fear? We were not entirely alone.

I was once again well provided with hot coals and blankets and flasks of tea. And, the gentleman before me...what had Father said? *Wanted to be married by Christmas...*

The colonel desired haste. Would there be time for love to grow? Perhaps that was a high expectation. My inner longing for such love had always been a hope I kept kindled. Did not every young woman?

I queried him, what did I have to lose? "I find I must ask you something, yet I do not mean to put you off."

He smiled from his corner. "I rather hoped we would be able to discuss—well—everything."

"You may think me foolish, but did you ever think to marry for...love?" He did not care about money, did he care about this? Did love matter to him? Heat rushed to my face as I realized to pertinent nature of my words.

"I don't think you foolish, Miss Chilton." He slipped his leather gloves from his hands, one finger at a time. "To answer your question, yes. I've every intention of marrying for love." The look he gave me sent a weakness to my knees.

I dared another question, my voice almost a whisper. "And how do you hope to accomplish so deep an emotion?" In so short a time...

"By deciding to love whom I have chosen." His voice had also gone a whisper.

"I see." I looked back to my hands but his firm voice rose.

"Miss Chilton, when I arrived in Bath, I had all but planned to abandon the idea and forego acquiring an introduction to you at the Assembly Ball. I paced the floor of my rooms until I knew naught except that I might as well catch a glimpse of you and then perhaps be introduced. Then, I would know for certain that I must not pursue you because you'd be all wrong. Like the women I had the misfortune to meet in London.

I'd envisioned a woman I probably couldn't abide." He laughed at the memory. "However, the Master of Ceremonies led me straight to you as though God had prompted him. I was entirely taken aback how it came about.

Then we danced, then I found myself leading you to supper—and you weren't some made-up tale by the vicar. But a real woman, the kind of whom both captivated and put my mind at ease. My purpose once again took root. Your humor and candor drew me in. Your uncle hadn't led me wrong. I found myself taking leave of you and not desiring to take my leave."

He'd revealed much. I swallowed at the whole of it. If only I had been privy to Uncle Harris' and my parent's machinations, I might have been—I don't know. Less stunned? "You are very honest sir."

Was his turn to ask. "Did you enjoy my company, too?" Hope lingered in his eyes.

I stifled a laugh. "When you left that night, I thought I'd never see you again."

His lips turned upward. "And yet, here we are."

"Yes. Here we are." A sudden shyness took over me. I wondered that Father did not reveal Colonel Stewart's identity to me at our discussion of my new course. Did he think I might not give him a chance?

We grew quiet and I observed his mended coat—the mark on his jaw had lightened considerably. "Whatever happened to your horse?"

He tensed and flashed his eyes to mine. "Stolen."

"You fought a man?"

"Miss Chilton, I would keep the unsavory details from your ears."

His tone had quite changed from gentle conversation we began with. But his words begged more questions. Did I really know who this man was, despite his honorable declarations—or my feelings.

"Unsavory details..." I repeated. "Please, you may trust me. I only hope no wrong has been done to you. I promise I am not the fainting type."

His jaw shifted as he considered what to tell. "I had some business to tend to on the way—let's just say that my presence was entirely unwelcome."

"I've never known business to come to fisticuffs..." A loss of fortune, to be sure, but fists and a stolen horse?

"Ah, certainly in the business of war—but war this was not, though I was ready to start a skirmish if need be. Turns out, the solicitor was not above board, cares little for the affairs of children, and will fight—aye—even steal my horse to ensure I understood that my wards will not receive an inheritance due them."

A crooked solicitor? "How can he prevent this?"

"To my shame, Andrew and Rachel have been at his mercy the year long while I was in Spain. I was informed a nursemaid cared for them and I was not to concern myself. As one who directs their affairs, I suspect the solicitor has misdirected the inheritance and now the children may have little to nothing left, aside from what I deem to provide."

"Theft?"

"The worst kind." He glanced from the window and turned back and observed me. "He assumed wrongly that I wanted nothing to do with the children. I tried for months to return to England, to be released of my command."

"Will nothing remain of their parent's estate?"

He shrugged his broad shoulders. "That is the question the solicitor danced around until he led me down a rabbit trail, attempting to entice me into a new speculation—no doubt planning to steal from me as well. Twas suspect. And when I confronted him, his assistant threw a fist to my jaw—quite out of the ordinary. One expects it on the battlefield, not in a solicitor's office."

"How very strange. What happened to the solicitor? Did you fight him?"

"The man grabbed a sheaf of papers and ran from the room, leaving me to fend for myself against the young brute."

"Such doings!"

"I have much to sort out after the holiday—when we—when I return to Highgate. Simon Smith must be held accountable."

"Simon Smith?" I'd heard the name many times. Was he not my Father's solicitor? Had he not been in Father's company that fateful day we lost everything? Due to Lord Banbury or some such man a few years dead? "You say one Simon Smith is solicitor to your wards?"

Colonel Stewart leaned forward. "Do you know the man?"

I shook my head. I did not know him per se. He'd been to dine with Father a time or two, twas all I knew. I feared I must confess it. "I do believe he is also my father's solicitor." I clenched my hands together. "I've only ever heard his name, mind you." I shifted in my seat, suddenly uncomfortable with the dismay written across Colonel Stewart's face. "On the day we discovered our losses—he was within our home—inside Father's office with a few other businessmen. I heard him speak...I..."

A smile quirked at his lips, the lift rather endearing. My, how my face flamed at every turn.

"You were eavesdropping?"

I glanced from the carriage window and back to him. "I didn't mean to do such a childish thing, only Mother knew nothing and I grew restless sitting in my room staring at four walls, waiting to fully understand what was happening to my family."

"I do not blame you. But," he took a breath and folded his arms. "Did your father tell you the reasons for his losses? Was Simon Smith involved?"

I licked my dry lips, desiring the flask of tea nestled within the basket. "I only know that Father has taken a great deal of guilt upon himself. I've never seen him so." In truth, the sadness that stretched across his face pained my heart more than I could bear. "He has begged our forgiveness time, and time again."

"Mmm."

I must make Colonel Stewart understand. Father was respectable in every way. "He has never known difficulty of this nature. Ever. His investments are always entirely above-board and—and—losh. What do I truly know? I am kept out of the details of his business. Only that you must believe that my Father is a man of honor."

Colonel Stewart bowed his head. "Of this I have no doubt, do not trouble yourself to save his reputation on my account. I spent an hour with him in his study after our assembly dance—tis when I gave him your uncle's letter."

Simon Smith—an unease filled my mind the same as it filled the carriage. The man all but had my would-be fiancé beaten. Stolen his horse—and mayhap mishandled an inheritance that didn't belong to him. What else had he done? Had he swindled my own father? "Did the constable help you, Colonel Stewart?"

He grimaced. "The constable and the magistrate were both deep in their cups, too inebriated to be of any use."

"What will you do next?"

He took a deep breath and tried to smile. "I will attempt to enjoy my holiday...our holiday. Handle this issue afterward." He shrugged his shoulders and held out his palms. "I would raise the children without what was left to them. Only their father died fighting for England. His earnings should be theirs."

I felt my father should be told. "Should we write to Father and tell him the man isn't to be trusted?"

Compassion now graced his eyes. "I do believe, forgive me, Miss Chilton, there is nothing left for the solicitor to assist him with or misappropriate. Your father has cut away from his business relations, all of them." He bowed his head with respect. "The Chilton's are penniless. Whether by way of this Simon Smith or not, your father understood that there was no recourse to the matter. Even if he did discover duplicity somewhere—as he has already questioned."

He was right. We were penniless. However, I pulled from my reticule a single pence and held it between us. "Only one remains." I don't know why, but I handed it to Colonel Stewart. "You are brave to desire wards as your own and to court a now penniless Chilton."

His eyes pierced mine as he took the pence and held it aloft in the light between us. He slowly pressed a kiss to the back of the coin. "You give me all you have; I will do the same for you." He pocketed the coin and gazed upon me until fire burned down to my toes.

I could not catch my breath, though immobile. I looked away, nestled in a corner, and did my best to sleep. Hours and hours of road remained...

Alone with this stranger who was determined to give me his heart.

Chapter Seven

I awoke to shouting. The carriage lurched and stopped a few times; I thought I had dreamt.

Colonel Stewart jostled my shoulder. "You must awake." His voice, tender.

I blinked at the darkness that had descended on the coach and shivered. "Are we at Uncle's? In Butterton?"

"Nay, we are not."

I sat up straight. The coals at my feet had cooled, and a shiver slipped around me.

"The road ahead of us is beset with brigands," He handed me my small satchel. "A passerby and his family have warned us. The poor wife is in shock as much of their belongings were stolen. Thank God they weren't wounded. The driver has found an inn—we must take shelter."

Brigands...highwaymen...thieves...I shuddered. Such were characters in novels. "Are we not but just over an hour's travel to Butterton?"

"Aye, we are. But the risk is too high." He reached over, unlatched the weapon box, and withdrew the pistol and leather pouch. "Do not concern yourself, tis only a precaution." He glanced behind him. "The driver has found an inn. We must take shelter. Tis not of the same caliber as you previously enjoyed. We'll be lucky to get a decent meal."

He opened the carriage door and helped me down. The inn was a bit ramshackle. But I felt safe with Colonel Stewart.

"Come." He led me into the place—only to discover one small room available. Men looked up from their cups and stared at us as though we intruded. Reminded me of sailors that sometimes descended upon Bath, of a sort I knew too well to keep away from. "Can't be helped," He whispered to my ear.

I cringed at my surroundings. The floors were dirty, the air smelled of beer and something sour I couldn't place.

We followed a woman who might have been the cook, for her apron was much stained, up a narrow flight of stairs and into the equally narrow room.

Colonel Stewart looked at me apologetically. "Miss Chilton, I cannot leave you here alone, defenseless. I won't do it." A spark lit his eyes.

I panicked at what he intimated. "I daresay we cannot continue our journey—not with brigands on the prowl." My heart thumped, and I swallowed, dearly wishing for a pot of tea and this impossible situation away from us.

"We cannot continue." His lips drew a line. He gazed at me, slowly blinking once. Willing me to understand.

I turned from him and fumbled with my gloves and hat. "My reputation..." I didn't know what to think or say. A single woman did not share a room with a gentleman. Ever.

I would never be trusted or looked well upon. Or befriended. The benefits of my acquaintance would be tainted. Mothers would draw their daughters away from me as I might influence them to the same reckless and irrecoverable behavior. There would never be a good enough excuse, though we had quite a legitimate one. The list grew. I'd chanced enough by riding in the carriage alone with him, despite the presence of the driver.

"Your reputation will not falter if I can help it. I would not do this if... dash it all." He jerked his coat off and tugged at his cravat and tossed them to a chair. I backed away—what did he do? A sudden dread snaked around my stomach. A gentleman did not disrobe before a lady...

"Your arrival to Butterton was to be one of ease! None of this discomfort and mayhem."

Mayhap, he did not think and was merely exhausted from these difficult days.

He paused, stepped close to me, and knelt; his collar hung open, revealing a portion of his chest—and another scar. Compassion replaced my dread. He had already endured difficulty. I might too...

He took my hand and squeezed it, gazing upon me with much sincerity. "For the manner in which I offer, I do greatly apologize. Will you, Miss Cassandra Chilton, consent to be my wife?"

My heart all but stopped because we must share a room. Word would fly among the villagers, from one to the next, of the pair that shared a space for the night. There would be no hiding such information from Uncle Harris once we arrived.

The village being so close to Butterton...we both knew the ramifications were steep.

I knew for certain within my heart of hearts. There was no conundrum. I did know my answer. From the moment I realized it was he who had sought my hand, I knew that I would agree to the match. I may as well accept now as would befit our circumstance.

"I will."

He rose and pressed a kiss to the back of my hand as he'd done the coin. "You do me great honor."

He gestured with his head towards the small bed. "Get some rest while I send for a vicar. We must marry now, not at Christmas as hoped. I will return momentarily. Indeed, I shall not even leave the top of the stairs."

"Now?"

He nodded. "Must be. Once again, this is not how I planned to take you as wife. I am more sorry than you can know."

"Will such vows be legal?"

"Ah." He pulled documents from his coat. "Special license."

Special license... Only those of high birth could possibly procure such.

"You..."

"Have friends in high places that owed me a favor."

Was I marrying a war hero of sorts? My goodness. One thing was certain. We wedded to save face. We could not be alone together in a bedchamber without vows forthcoming. Colonel Stewart dashed into the hall and shouted for a servant and returned to me in a moment. He re-tied his cravat and put his coat back on.

My heart began to thud erratically. I stood in front of the old, spotted mirror that hung on the wall. My hair fell in sections from my chignon and lacked the stylish curls by my cheeks that I was rather known to wear. With nervous fingers, I did what I could to straighten the mess. I had little experience and no Lila to help me rearrange my hair.

My hand trembled as I tried to pin a section away from my face. I dropped it.

"Here. Let me." Colonel Stewart. He retrieved the pin and stilled, his hands paused around my face. "I don't want you to be afraid. Are you afraid?"

I licked my lips. "I'm trying not to be."

He took a section of my hair and twisted it, angling the pin just so as to capture the wild tresses. He did so again. When he was finished, he backed away. "You are a beautiful bride."

He meant to put me at ease, make me feel lovely on the cusp of my vows to him. But he continued to gaze with those warm, brown eyes of his. "I am so very sorry. I desired haste, but not quite so sudden..."

"You've naught to apologize for." Had not every event come of a sudden? Was there no stopping these life-changing waves? But instead of being assaulted by them, I was invigorated by the newness of my situation, as though I were being dashed awake to the real world and real living. Made my previous pampered life seem altogether boorish. Yet, true, I was a mite afraid. And nervous. Most brides had months to prepare. I had, as of this morning, but ten days—and now? An hour at the most.

A knock came to the door.

"Are you ready?" Colonel Stewart held out his arm.

I couldn't stop trembling. "I am." I took his arm, and the vicar led us down a muddy lane to the front of the shadowed altar, where his wife and another witness waited in the tiny, dimly lit church.

We joined ungloved hands, his—strong and calloused with the work of the call to arms. We repeated our vows slowly. He, as though he'd waited a long time to say them and wanted to mean them. I then repeated those sacred words in the same way.

Having been overlooked the few Seasons I enjoyed, I found this marriage to be nothing short of miraculous. I hoped, with a mildly sick feeling, that he wouldn't regret it—and I wouldn't either. One simply did not abandon a marriage. Colonel Stewart slipped a ring on my finger—a simple band of gold.

The vicar announced a kiss. Did he assume ours a marriage of passion? Before I could think, Colonel Stewart placed a hand on my cheek and settled a feathery soft kiss upon my lips. Mayhap...mayhap it would be.

The vicar made sure our union was properly recorded, officially signing the license. A dip of the quill into ink by a flickering candle dripping wax in a stream down a short lectern, the soft laugh of his wife serenading like a song...our names were forever linked.

The vicar admonished us. "Better than a wedding by an anvil-priest, mind you. Hold to your vows, hold to each other.

You have done no frivolous thing. By every means, hold to God, Mr. and Mrs. Stewart."

Colonel Stewart held my hand fast. "We intend to do so."

"I shall be writing to Vicar Harris so that he may receive confirmation beyond your word of the validity of your union. He and I are good friends." He placed a hand on either of our shoulders. "My wife and I will see you back to the inn. Do be careful on the rest of your journey."

The cold walk through the village to the inn was made warmer by what I'd just done. I'd just vowed myself to this man for life, as long as I would live it. While our action had been an appropriate response to our situation, I felt anything but at ease. My nerves soared. I was married. To one whom I was undeniably attracted to yet had not grown to love. Or had I?

Did not his gentle words about choosing to love whom he had chosen melt the heart of me? His eyes, his care, his thoughtfulness. His plan to make more of his wards than an obligation spoke deeply of this man's character.

I looked up at him and found he looked down upon me. "You are tired."

"Ever so much."

"Mrs. Stewart?"

It took a split second to realize my new title. "Yes?"

"May I call you Cassandra?"

"Please do." The way he said my name—indeed, I was beginning to love the very sound of his voice. I'd lost my head. Moonstruck, no doubt.

"You may call me Nathan. No more addressing me as "colonel", if you please. I am not your commander."

Soon, we'd said a final goodnight to the vicar and his wife and made our way back to the tiny bedroom. Just as a new fear surged, Colonel Stewart—Nathan—held up his hands. "You must be well rested for your reunion with your family tomorrow. You'll take the bed, and I will rest by the door." He retrieved the pistol again and inspected it.

He would be uncomfortable...but...we could not...I...nerves fluttered and abounded. I could scarcely remove my cloak for the knot in the ties. He set the pistol down and approached me as he had when I dropped my hairpin.

"I intend," he removed my hands from fighting the knot and placed his hands on my shoulders, "to love my wife in the best way possible. You must not be afraid, Cassandra. I understand that we hardly know each other, but I shall enjoy discovering who you are with time."

I blinked away an errant tear. He swiped it away with a stroke of his thumb. "Everything...with time. We need not hurry those things even though our marriage had to be rushed."

His brown eyes glistened in the dark, single candle-lit room. The flame offered little, yet I burned the brighter within when I took in the scar that peeked up from his cravat, the set of his lips, the wave in his sandy hair.

His purpose was unlike any man I'd ever known or expected. It fit with my recent revelation about my own life. We were meant to be.

He loosened the knot and drew my cloak from my shoulders. Something else loosened within me as well.

"Good night, Cassandra." He stepped away and turned his back before hunching down upon the hard floor.

I sat upon the narrow bed and blew out the flame, yet it did not die within me. I lay there and watched the back of him until my eyelids drooped.

Chapter Eight

I received a kiss on my cheek when waking. Nathan knelt beside the bed and rubbed my shoulder. "Time you wake, Cassandra."

I blinked and sat up. Nathan smiled, and I remembered. I was his wife. I looked down at the ring on my hand and recounted the vows but hours long.

He donned his coat. "We arrive in Butterton this morning! We shall be much safer in the daylight. I know you are anxious to see your family and me, my wards." He stopped short. "Our wards."

The children to whom I was to be a mother. Another occupation I'd yet to fathom.

We alighted the carriage after breakfasting on watery porridge with no cream, but thankfully, the tea was extra strong. As a result, I felt much revived.

The hour passed swiftly, amicably. I caught him smiling more than a few times while looking in my direction. I might confess to doing the same. I believed ourselves to be made happy by our suddenly married state.

At long last, the driver stopped before the old rectory. Nathan opened the door. "What's this?" A horse stood tied to the post. "My horse. How on earth…" He reached for me and looked about. No one but villagers about their duties.

The door to the rectory stood open. I ran towards it. "Uncle?" Nathan came behind me.

"Uncle Harris?" We searched the house. It was empty. Near the back, a crock of pickles had dropped to the flagstone floor and shattered to pieces. The tang of vinegar filled the air. A doll lay amid the puddle.

Nathan picked it up. "Tis Rachel's."

The driver hauled in my trunks, and Nathan ran to his horse and checked the saddle bags. "Nothing missing. Only, there's this." He lifted an envelope from the pouch with his name scrawled upon it. He ripped it open, withdrew the message, and read aloud.

Colonel Stewart,

Your horse was discovered abandoned and walking without his rider along the path behind the wash house. It was directed that you'd lost control of him due to an unfortunate unseating and from your abusive use of the whip.

Bear in mind that valued possessions can be taken at any time when that possession isn't handled correctly.

I return your horse to you in good faith that you will take me at my word.

Simon Smith, Esq.

"He was here. How did he know my destination?" Nathan looked around once again. A crack split the air as a whoosh sped between us. Nathan grabbed me and pulled me down. "Run to the house, quick."

We scrambled inside. He bolted the door, dragging me with him to bolt the back door too. "Dear God," He uttered as he snatched the carriage pistol he'd kept and loaded it quickly. "Sit down—there." He gestured to a chair.

"I can't." I trembled from head to toe. "What is happening?"

"I've been shot at."

Never had I...I licked my lips. Where was Uncle Harris? His wife and the children?

A low fire still snapped in the kitchen hearth. Christmas greens lay across the table as though the children had been helping twine them together. Spiced cookies cut in the shape of people lay on a plate, one half eaten.

Nathan went from window to window, spying, watching. Waiting. It was just after midday, was it not? I don't know how long we waited before I heard Nathan cock the pistol. He looked at me and held a finger to his lips and shooed me to hide from view. I did as told.

A knock sounded at the door.

Nathan paused, uncertain.

"Colonel Stewart, sir? Miss Chilton? Are you within?" The voice sounded young. "I am Matthew Dawes, and I have with me Joseph Carter. If you can hear me, and don't mind, do open the door."

Nathan refused with a shake of his head.

The young voice continued. "I am from Lord Sherborne of Goodwyn Abbey. We are here to assist."

I heard Nathan open the door on squeaky hinges.

I tightened my grip on the chair in front of me. Would there be a fight? And why?

Another voice joined in. "You've naught to fear, Colonel. With all due respect, if I wanted to take you out, I could have done so already."

Nathan repeated the man's name. "You are *that* Joseph Carter?" Nathan opened the door wider but kept the pistol positioned. I slipped from my hiding place to watch.

The men bowed to him. The young man called Matthew continued, "Lord Sherborne sent us to assist you. It seems the vicar had some trouble this morning. They were concerned about whether you should arrive and find them missing."

Mr. Carter looked at the pistol Nathan held and closed the door behind them. "Seems like you may have had trouble as well."

Nathan lowered the gun, and I stepped beside him. "We arrived to find my recently stolen horse delivered here—and no sign of the vicar or his wife, as you say. Broken crockery in the kitchen. When we were outside, I was shot at."

Matthew and Mr. Carter exchanged glances.

Mr. Carter stepped towards me. "You are Miss Chilton? I am pleased to make your acquaintance." He bowed. "Matthew?"

The youth bowed as well. "Pleased, Miss."

Nathan corrected them. "Tis Mrs. Stewart now. And I am glad you have come." He bolted the door once again. "What sort of mischief occurred this morning?"

Mr. Carter's brows rose. "Seems the headmaster of a boy's school, one of ill repute, had been sent to collect the boy. The order had been signed by you, purportedly. The disagreement between the vicar and said headmaster resulted in a scuffle where the good wife took the children and locked themselves in the church until the vicar was released of the vile man."

Matthew added to the story. "Vicar knew you hadn't signed the order. Knew your plans to provide his education yourself—and knew the school wasn't fit for any child to live in."

"Simon Smith…" The name left my lips, and three sets of eyes rested upon me.

Mr. Carter banked the coals still lit in the parlor hearth with a shovel.

Matthew asked, "Who is this Smith fellow? The headmaster's name?"

Nathan folded his arms. "No, I think not."

Mr. Carter rose. "Let us begone from here with all haste. Lord Sherborne awaits us at Goodwyn, where your uncle and the children have taken shelter." He looked at me. "Gather what you can carry in a small bag from your trunk, and we shall escort you to Goodwyn."

I did as told while the men looked from the windows and waited.

I cleared my throat. "Are you sure it's safe?"

"Safer now than later." Mr. Carter looked at Nathan. "Wouldn't you agree, Colonel?"

He assented. "I will follow the word of the man who trained some of my best infantrymen." He gave a nod. "Lead on."

We exited the house as Matthew continued to look in all directions. Two horses were tied next to Nathan's.

"Pardon, Mrs. Stewart. The best way to get to Goodwyn quickly is to ride. No carriage. Can you manage?"

"I've not ridden in ages."

Nathan had already mounted and reached for me. Mr. Carter put his hands together to launch me up. "Here we go!"

Nathan pulled me by the waist and nestled me close to him. Matthew and Mr. Carter swung into their saddles.

Mr. Carter instructed Matthew. "You take the front, no, do as I say, Dawes." He turned his horse around. "I will be at the back of you. Keep a good pace. Ready?"

I was pressed so close to Nathan's heart that I felt it thrumming into my back. His pulse and mine raced with the fear of what evil might give chase and what chance we might have together. *God, keep us in your care...*

We kept a good trot for only a few minutes before we reached a country road, and just then, another crack popped behind us. Mr. Carter yelled an order. "Charge to Goodwyn!"

I tried to look. "No, Cassandra," Nathan ordered. He kicked his horse beneath us and shouted as we sped behind Matthew, Nathan's body leaning forward, my own pressed tightly onto the beast's neck.

It was some minutes before Mr. Carter shouted for us to slow our pace. The road that stretched before us was surrounded by wide open hills, and the estate that must be Goodwyn Abbey was positioned at the end of it.

Mayhap, the brigands that beset the road to Butterton last eve were the same that desired to threaten Nathan. Had they lain in wait for him? Only to find we did not pass that way as expected?

I thought back to the man who had warned our driver to halt for the night. Who was he? Did these men make themselves out to be highwaymen only, or were they truly Simon Smith and his thugs? Yet if a thief is a thief in one way, why not the other? Did greedy men forever desire gain?

Another thought pummeled my mind. My father had been tricked out of our fortune—it had been stolen. If Simon Smith had dared write a note such as he'd left for Nathan, what else had he done and what was he doing now?

How strange that the man was involved in both of our lives...

Closer and closer, we careened towards safety. We drew the notice of men with firearms that seemed to parol the grounds—they sent a salute to Mr. Carter. What kind of man was he? Had he really trained some of Nathan's men?

Nathan had straightened and pulled me up against him. He murmured in my ear. "Not exactly the romantic ride I envisioned having with you."

A shocked giggle rose from my throat.

"Rest assured, we shall have one."

"Colonel Stewart—Nathan..."

"Are you well, Cassandra? I'm sorry you had to go through that. I never realized obtaining children and a wife could incite such danger."

"I am well, only concerned. The children must be frightened."

"Mm. Yes. I wish it weren't so."

We drew beneath a portico, and the stablemaster helped me down from the saddle. A gentleman stood tall and mildly foreboding, his hands clutched behind his back.

The man stepped forward as Nathan dismounted. "Long have I desired to meet one of the heroes of Albuera."

Nathan jerked his head. "A useless, costly failure."

"In which your intelligent actions saved more than one life." Lord Sherborne bowed. "You must know that we wrestle not against flesh and blood, but against principalities, against powers, against the rulers of the darkness of this world, against spiritual wickedness in high places…" His brows rose. "Betimes a win looks like a loss."

The man turned to me and bowed. "Miss Chilton, you are most welcome to Goodwyn. Your uncle will be relieved you've arrived."

A door opened behind him, and we were ushered into the ancient hall. Much happened all at once. Uncle's arms were embracing me; children had tackled Nathan, one around his neck, the other wrapped around his leg. Just as they might a father…

I was introduced to Uncle's wife, Margaret, whose kindness knew no bounds. We were steered into a comfortable parlor where fresh pots of tea had been delivered and poured out by Lady Sherborne herself.

Christmas greens had been hung about the room, and bundles of bright-berried holly in silver cups were on nearly every surface. Newspaper roses, an odd decoration to be sure, were gathered in bouquets in grand assortments, with greenery tucked amongst the flowers.

Clove-studded oranges scented the air. Twas Christmas here. I allowed myself a moment alone by the bright hearth. To think, so much had happened in under a month's time—and even more within a few days. I swallowed the hot, creamy tea, and swallowed more, taking in both my surroundings and circumstances.

All were shocked to learn of our marriage, and many congratulations went around. Uncle Harris was mildly miffed. "I was to oversee the ceremony. Indeed." He sipped his tea. "But well done all the same."

Nathan joined me by the hearth and spoke in a private tone. "I worry for you. Shall I ask for you to be led to your room? We are to remain here until the danger is passed, I'm told."

It was true. The horse ride with my husband had quite stolen my breath, but so did the way the handsome man looked at me in concern.

Uncle Harris guffawed. "There's no stopping a gentleman when he wants a bride, eh, Lady Sherborne? Mrs. Carter?"

I looked at the good-natured women who sat nearby on a settee, both smiling. I sensed a story there.

The one called Elaina spoke. "You aren't the first bride to require a swift marriage." She glanced at Lord Sherborne, who looked upon his wife with unhindered affection.

Mr. Carter's wife, Emmaline, agreed. "Indeed. Nor are you the first to lose a fortune and run from danger."

Elaina patted the seat next to her, and I sat. "Too bad Ewan and Jane aren't here. They would also be in good company. However, I do wonder when the ruling over Butterton Hall will ever come in Jane's favor. Perhaps they might join us for the holiday next year."

I accepted another cup of tea. "This Jane, she also married in haste?"

Elaina nodded and spoke in a quiet voice. "Life runs a different path when one puts one's life in the hands of God. He won't lead us wrong, even if the path is to the altar and love is yet to grow."

"I thank you for that. I've only just begun to realize what true living may be outside of parties and dances—and what gentleman my life would be joined with to perpetuate the same."

She smiled. "You sound like Emmaline, in a way."

Emmaline leaned forward. "I wouldn't trade my dear cottage for all the estates in England."

Mr. Carter folded his arms. "I thought you loved me more than my cottage."

She laughed. "Nearly as much."

Mr. Carter smiled. "Will be a good place to raise our children..."

A hand slipped over her waist. "Yes."

I'd witnessed a private moment and knew—she was with child.

And thinking of children, a noise rustled through the door. What had Nathan said their names were? Rachel and... A tall, youthful man bounded after them, grinning and laughing. The children pulled each of his hands and the younger, Rachel, held a paper rose bouquet.

The boyish man giggled as they approached. They stood in a row before me as little Rachel spoke. "Roses for the bride." She handed them to me while the man clapped his hands. The boy smirked.

Lady Sherborne rose—and Nathan joined me.

"Mrs. Stewart, this is Callum. He is a master of crafting paper roses and all manner of flowers, are you not?"

Callum laughed again and bounded from the room.

Nathan put a hand on the children's shoulder. "Rachel, Andrew, this is my wife. Cassandra, Rachel, and Andrew have been anxious to make your acquaintance."

The girl stumbled a curtsy, and the boy offered a sheepish bow.

Andrew leaned in and observed my face. "You look nothing like our mother. I hoped you would not."

"Andrew." Nathan's voice, while stern, held an edge of compassion.

Andrew stepped back.

I needed to reassure him. "It is alright. I am not offended. Your mother must have been very beautiful." I could tell by the fine features of the children. She truly must have been.

"You are very nice too." Rachel poked at one of the flowers. "I made that one."

"I thank you both." I offered what I hoped was a warm smile. "I look forward to knowing you better."

Rachel giggled and Andrew pulled her hand as they ran from the room. Callum's laugh joined theirs in the hall. The youthful man seemed to make a good playmate.

Lord Sherborne laughed after them. "Callum will sleep well tonight, I think."

A sudden wave of emotion hit me just then. Those beautiful children were to be under my care. A sense of protective love rose from within me—a kind of love I didn't know I had. So different than what I thought I'd feel about being a governess, merely working on behalf of the mother. Nay, I was to be as like a mother as possible. Daunting, to be sure, yet sacred.

A tear slipped down my cheek. I could not stop the flow.

Nathan pulled me to my feet. "I must beg your pardon, Lady Sherborne. My bride must rest."

"Of course. Let me show you to your rooms."

We followed her through the aged hall of high, stained glass windows and arches, up the stairs, and to a suite of rooms.

She paused and opened a door. "We thought you'd like the blue rooms." She handed me an extra handkerchief. "Shall I ring for a bath to be brought?"

Nathan answered for me. "I think that is best."

She pulled the bell. "I'll have more tea sent up as well. I daresay you might prefer to dine in your private parlor together tonight—tomorrow, you will feel more yourselves."

"You are too kind." I managed.

We dined, I bathed, and we slept in our respective rooms. Such was the first day as Mrs. Nathan Stewart.

Chapter Nine

I slept soundly—no dreams beset my rest. But I woke to a nagging question. What were we to do? It was now but a week before Christmas, the time had been intended to get to know Colonel Stewart, and by way of difficulty, I had already married him.

What would Mother and Father think of the predicaments I'd found myself in?

A maid helped me don a fresh gown and plaited my hair into a coronet.

Would we remain in Butterton as planned? Should we, if danger lurked here? I opened the door to our small common parlor and found Nathan standing before the fire.

"Good morning, Cassandra." He approached and bent to place a light kiss on my cheek that left a trail of fire. My, but he was handsome.

Did he feel the burn as I did? I knew he had chosen to love me, but did he feel a flicker of passion? I flushed at my own thoughts.

Breakfast had been delivered to the table just under the window. Nathan pulled my chair. "Lord Sherborne states we must reside here for a few days at least, then we may return to the vicarage and enjoy our holiday as planned."

"What does Simon Smith play at, I wonder? Does he desire to retain control of the children's welfare?"

"I believe he is most interested in their inheritance, which may already be gone. If the children disappear, then the inheritance, what is left..." He shook his head. "I do not know. Only that Lieutenant Watson should never have trusted the man with his affairs. I suppose I should be glad he named me caretaker of his children."

"You knew their father?"

"I knew him well." He paused with his fork in the air and lowered it. "Died in battle."

"I sense he was a friend."

He took a deep breath. "A most trusted friend. Yes."

"No wonder you are invested in the children's upbringing."

"Their father saved my life. Not once, but twice. If only I had saved him as well, the children wouldn't be without parents. He was the best of men."

I couldn't fathom being raised without my own dear mother and father. They were all I had. "Rachel and Andrew shall have us..."

The corners of his mouth lifted. "Us. Yes." He reached for my hand and slipped his fingers between mine. "I rather like how we are turning out." He gazed at me with a gentleness that I'd experienced before. "We are a pair."

My pulse raced. I looked down at our entwined fingers, the band of gold declaring it to be forever true.

"Cassandra, I am as stunned at our circumstances as you are. But a few months ago, I'd only begun entertaining the idea of taking a wife. After I prayed about it, I knew I must." He shook his head. "I just didn't know how such a miracle would come about. Or that the vicar had a great-niece—or that when I met her, I would be so instantly taken with her. Or that strange circumstances would force the deed done." He stroked my hand with his thumb. "I'm sorry for the hard parts, but I can't apologize for our marriage."

Had I known that Father's hardships would turn my life toward something greater and better—I would have spent the better part of my discouragement on my knees instead of wringing my hands at our losses.

Here was a great gain. Simon Smith may have tried to ruin Father—would I ever know? Had tried to interfere with Andrew and Rachel's lives. No matter the thefts, we would have each other. We would choose to love.

"What is it, Cassandra?"

Oh, the way he said my name. "I am thinking that God has given me much good out of an impossible problem…"

"He sees what we cannot. Knows the difference between what is fair and what is best…and the kind of happiness we would prefer if we left our destinations up to Him."

I noted the scar that snaked over his collar. His destination had been battle, a real battle where his life had not only been at stake but had been rescued. Much of what he'd endured certainly was not fair. Nay, he'd met with evil in all of its fierceness. Yet he was able to speak of God's best with the sound of experience.

"I am to meet with Lord Sherborne as soon as we have breakfasted." He removed his hand, and I felt the loss. "Mr. Smith may have misappropriated the children's inheritance for his own gain, but there's one thing it cannot do is truly benefit him."

"I can almost pity the wretch."

"I suppose I'd allow for pity once he is caught. Or whoever it was that shot at me yesterday. In truth, I can think of no other reason than he still desires control over the children to retain control of the funds. There must be a portion left, or why bother? If I am out of the way, he becomes the legal overseer."

I managed to eat some toast and egg, down some hot coffee with rich cream. I felt more myself in that moment than I believe I ever had. I was in the right place at the right time. Regardless of the danger. If Nathan had endured it, so could I.

He pulled my chair and lifted me to my feet. "Let us join the others, shall we?"

We both paused, my hand still in his. The air grew scarce in my lungs. He bent his head and leaned in as the door opened. I startled.

A maid. "Pardon me, Mr. Stewart. Mrs. Stewart. I'll just take the breakfast things if you are finished?"

Nathan put space between us. "We are quite finished." He tucked my hand into his arm and led me from the room.

Had he been about to kiss me? We were married. It would be assumed that such affection would grow between us. But I well knew how a single spark led to a blazing fire. The few times his lips had softly grazed my hand, cheek, and even my lips when we'd said our vows, I'd nearly buckled.

I would seem forward if I showed much desire. Was it forward if we were married?

I spent the remainder of the morning with Uncle Harris and his wife inside a rather cozy library with a fire built high. We'd much to catch up on as it had been many months since I'd spoken with him.

Uncle Harris patted my hand. "The Weatherington's are well known and liked. I do hope your parents will be happily employed there."

"Father seemed relieved to be given the position, and they are good friends after all."

"And we equally hope you will be happy with Colonel Stewart?" He looked concerned. "You'd a hasty wedding, with little time to get to know him. You were supposed to have a few weeks and a little more time to decide. Appears God decided for you. How do you feel about that?"

Gracious, my uncle was forthcoming. "I can honestly tell you that I've never felt more at ease in anyone's company. Not even Susan Richards..." Or a ball of nerves, or so aflame... but this I would never confess.

"Ah, this is how it is." He took his wife's hand. "Margaret and I felt much the same upon our meeting, did we not?"

She laughed. "I never thought to marry until he walked through my door."

Uncle Harris's smile widened. "If you both desire it, your love will blossom overnight." He winked. "I rather think it already has."

"Uncle!"

"No shame, my dear. God created romance with all of its facets, and we must not be ashamed to feel these things He created us to feel, without restraint."

"I believe in your case, my dear vicar, some restraint might be needed upon occasion." His wife chided.

He released a great guffaw. "I kissed her before the lady's circle last week and stunned them to silence. Including Margaret."

She rolled her eyes. "King Solomon in all his glory..."

"Boasted far more than I, the rascal." He slipped an arm around her shoulders and grinned at me.

I didn't know where to look. "I think I must give you privacy this very moment." I dashed from the room to his laughter chasing my back.

The next words I heard rather stopped me in my tracks. The drawing room door had been left open, and men's voices came from the other side.

Lord Sherborne spoke. "What will you do when you return?"

Nathan responded, "You may think me daft."

"You don't strike me as a simple-minded man."

"Indeed, mayhap a lovestruck one." Nathan was lovestruck? I covered my mouth.

"In love with your wife already?" Lord Sherborne's voice tinged with humor.

"I cannot help it. Never did I believe in love at first sight. Thought it but Cupid's myth."

"Until you saw her—and you knew, didn't you? As though an arrow had pierced your heart through?"

"She may think me mad if I tell her such."

"Must you tell her?"

Silence. He was in love with me? And not just choosing to be?

Lord Sherborne cleared his throat. "Would you believe me if I told you I experienced nearly the same strong emotion? I saw Elaina, and it was as though God Himself had stamped her image on my heart."

Nathan spoke. "Indeed. As soon as I dined with Cassandra—and escorted her home, every protective instinct rose within me. I couldn't sleep. Couldn't rest. And when I hired the best possible carriage to deliver her to Butterton, I planned to follow some paces behind. A good thing I did. Or—" he paused.

"Ah, we mustn't think about the what-ifs. Doesn't help. She is safely yours."

Urgency tinted Nathan's voice. "I had not planned that danger would beset our path."

Lord Sherborne agreed. "I don't think anyone plans that." Footsteps shuffled across the floor. "I shall hie to my study and peruse my papers and affidavits from the Banbury case—I'm certain I've heard the name of Simon Smith before. Could be something there to help you."

I turned around and made as though I'd just come upon them and entered the doorway.

"Cassandra." Nathan smiled.

Lord Sherborne bowed. "If you will excuse me. I will let you know if I find out anything. Joseph Carter, Matthew, and a few other men are scoping out the village and surrounding areas for any unusual arrivals. Hopefully, the threat, whoever it is, will do us a favor and cease his harassments for the holiday—if not indefinitely."

Nathan agreed. "One can hope."

Lord Sherborne left us alone.

Nathan's brows rose. He folded his arms and confronted me. "How much did you hear?"

My head bent in shame even as a betraying smile raised my lips.

He stepped to me, bringing his hand under my chin and lifting my face to look at him. He tried a rather militant voice. "I await an answer."

The handsome cut of his jaw, his wavy, sandy hair. The lines that bespoke days of hard living, the scar that I'd yet to fully know...his eyes—melted the whole of me. He saw the truth. I'd heard his words but dared not shame him for it. Indeed, no...

His hand stayed beneath my chin, the other slipping to my back and ever so gently pulling me forward. His eyes asked the question, nay, begged an answer. I blinked slowly, suddenly unable to think.

He dipped his head closer to mine and angled his face. A whisper of a kiss met my lips and stayed. The first kiss—a spark, the next a flame. My hands crept up his chest as his other hand pressed me closer to him, the next kiss afire.

One would think we were starved for this kind of affection, mayhap we were. He put his hands on either side of my face and whispered my name. "Cassandra...you have my heart."

"Colonel Nathan Stewart, you have mine."

He bent and kissed me again, then held me close to his chest.

I pitied the Season's debutantes. The many young ladies. Susan Richards...they may never know such a love as mine. Then I prayed for them, that a sort of revolution would come upon the hearts of the ton, that they might choose to love as Nathan and I had done, that God might smite their hearts open to such compassion and passion.

"I hate to break the newlyweds apart, but Colonel Stewart, I find a strong reason for us to ride to Simon Smith's office and pay him a rather special visit."

I stepped from Nathan's embrace to see Lord Sherborne with a sheaf of papers in his hands.

An hour later, Nathan kissed my hand and rode away. "I'll be but a few days at the most, Sherborne says."

Elaina and I waved to them.

Kissing hadn't satisfied me. No. It only woke a longing for more, for his arms to ever be about me. I was not prepared, though I be his wife for under two days, to be separated from him. No matter how short a time it was to be.

Chapter Ten

I spent idle hours helping Elaina and Emmaline wrap gifts for the tenants who lived on Goodwyn's land. It was festive work involving tissue and satin ribbon that the girls would undoubtedly wear in their hair all year long.

I was not accustomed to the idea of tenants, though I believed Nathan had them. I plied Elaina to teach me how to go about being a proper mistress of such a living. How I might do good to those dependent on Nathan's land.

The hours sped by, night fell, and morning came. Three days had passed, and still, Nathan and Lord Sherborne had yet to return.

I played games with the children when they could be coaxed from Callum's side, and of an evening, and read aloud fairy tales from a book I'd enjoyed as a child.

They were lively, sweet, and rambunctious and gave me a glimpse of what my life would be like when we made Nathan's estate a home for us all. I wondered what Highgate looked like, how far away...

Mr. Carter and Matthew took Andrew aside and gave him his first fencing lesson while we watched his moves and clapped at his valor. Confidence replaced the boyish smirk, and I could see the man he would become.

Uncle Harris and Margaret were given leave by Mr. Carter to return to the vicarage to put it back to rights and prepare for me and the children to join them the next day.

Twas but two more days until Christmas. Snow began to fall, white, thick, and crisp. Mr. Carter helped the children and me into the carriage with our things and rode behind so that I might feel at ease. By the time we arrived at the vicarage and Mr. Carter had taken his leave, snow already measured so deep, I worried Nathan wouldn't be able to return at all.

What if evil had befallen him? And Lord Sherborne?

The children and I baked gingerbread men with Margaret, helped set the pudding to steam, and brined a small turkey while Uncle Harris prepared for Christmas services. We were busy, but the loneliness in my heart stretched as wide and far as Nathan was gone from my side.

I worried. Tomorrow was Christmas Eve.

Andrew tugged at my elbow. "When is Colonel Stewart coming back?"

"Soon, I hope."

Fear rested behind his eyes. And I realized. He had awaited his own father's return—but he'd died in battle. Distress pricked.

"We shall pray for him and Lord Sherborne, yes? No doubt they are delayed by this snow."

He nodded and chased off after his sister. My chin trembled, and Margaret came to my side and took my hand. She bowed her head and prayed for Nathan and Lord Sherborne's safety—her words soothed. Never before had I understood how much I needed to talk to God before my troubles—and blessings—began.

I was not to worry much longer. I had just opened a book to read when the door to the vicarage opened and in walked Nathan. My husband...

I am not ashamed to say that I ran straight into his arms. He held me tight and kissed my face as though I were a long-lost love. May it never be.

We drew apart, and I poured him a cup of tea. "What did you find?"

Nathan shook his head. "Absolutely nothing. When we arrived, Simon Smith's office had been entirely vacated. Every scrap of paper was gone from the place. We followed a few leads to no avail. Yet, Lord Sherborne bears an affidavit that he was involved in one of Banbury's speculating schemes—apart from stealing from Andrew and Rachel."

"Indeed?"

"Lord Sherborne believes it was his own scheme that ruined your father, not Banbury's." He swallowed more tea and closed his eyes. "The man tried to mimic his predecessor, all told. If done badly."

"Father is usually a good judge of character."

"Some gentlemen are quite good at posturing a business proposition that is a mere façade. When other good businessmen are involved and add to the influence, it can be hard to see the lies."

He placed an arm around my shoulders and leaned in. "I hated being apart from you."

The children ran into the room just then and bounded upon his lap. I spied Andrew swiping a tear from his eye. The poor soul had lost far too much for one so young.

We gathered for a cozy meal that evening. Uncle Harris blessed the food and the six of us partook of a simple stew and hot rolls.

Uncle Harris and Margaret retired early, and Nathan and I tucked the children into their beds together. Familial bliss, a moment that will forever be marked in my memory. Watching him pull the covers over Rachel's sweet, little form. The salute he gave to Andrew...

The boy whispered to me when I knelt by his side and stroked a lock of hair from his eyes. "I'm glad you are come."

"I am too."

He smiled as his eyes fluttered with sleep.

Nathan took my hand and blew out the chamber stick.

A mere taste of what our lives would be had changed me in a moment.

Nathan led me from the room and to the highbacked bench beside the fire. He took my face between his hands and kissed me as softly as before. And again—was love so rich? He kissed my temples, my jaw. I tugged at his cravat, unknotting it at his throat, and slipped it away from his neck. There was the scar.

I pulled back the fabric and traced my finger along the line, but the line did not stop where the shirt remained buttoned. My heart thumped as I chanced a look at his eyes. He kissed my forehead. He drew back, but I drew close—and kissed the scar at his collarbone.

"How bad was it?" I whispered.

"It doesn't hurt any longer." He drew my lips back to his, and time passed. The clock chimed midnight. He scooted away and held out his hands. "Retire, Cassandra." As tired as his voice sounded, yet there was a command about it.

I did not want to leave him. I knew he did not want to leave me. I felt some shame at being pushed away.

He took both of my hands in his. "I would see my bride installed on my estate..."

"I see."

"I would court my wife on Christmas week. May I have this honor?"

"You may."

"Good." He pressed another kiss to my forehead.

Festivities began tomorrow—and Nathan had returned in time. For this, I was thankful.

I made for the stairs just as I heard door hinges squeak. A blast of cold crept at my ankles. I turned, and I heard a click.

A stranger had entered the room. Someone had forgotten to bolt the front door. Simon Smith held a pistol before Nathan. I swallowed a scream for fear he'd shoot.

"Run, Cassandra." Nathan bit out the words, but all I could do was back weakly against the wall. I could not leave him.

"If it isn't the Chilton miss. What scandal shall reach the ears in Bath soon, eh?"

Nathan growled. "What do you want with me?"

"I want you to resign your rights to the children."

"No."

"Shame it has to come to this."

"Why care you for the children?"

"I don't." The solicitor stepped closer to Nathan. "You were supposed to die in the Peninsula."

"Was I indeed? I'm glad you are not God that you can choose."

Mr. Smith laughed at that. "Would that God held the gun and I did not." His lips curved back into a straight line. "I can indeed choose to kill you."

"If you kill me, you think the children will be yours to do with and none to discover what you did with their inheritance? Is that it?"

"How astute." He sneered. "And what does a young single Colonel desire with children? Naught but a burden."

Nathan flicked his chin. "You've lost your mind. You'd never get away with it."

"Won't I?"

"Someone is after you, is that it? The late Lord Banbury has double-crossed you, and you've been double-crossing everyone else to pay your own debts. You must be running out of time if you are desperate enough to come after mere children."

Mr. Smith did not reply but cocked the pistol and aimed.

My vision blackened. A shot was fired, then another, but I fell into a heap on the floor.

A scream, a shout, and voices rang about my head. Visions ran in short clips in my mind.

"I've got him, he's down."

Yes, no. Take her.

Palms slapped my cheeks. Tears flowed. Nathan.

Strong arms lifted me. Nathan. Nathan lifted me. Another man joined him. Others. I blinked to reality. I was in my room.

"He's deceased. Colonel Stewart." Mr. Carter plunged inside, red-cheeked and cross-strapped with a long rifle and powder horn, a pistol still in his grip. "Man lost his mind!"

Mr. Carter. He'd come. Had he shot him?

I looked to Nathan who still held me. "You aren't wounded?"

"No, my love." He looked back to Mr. Carter. "How did you know to come?"

"I've been tracking him since you returned. Sherborne had a keen sense you both were being followed and thought it wouldn't hurt to send men out to be certain." He shook his head. "The man was a fool to come back. Utterly careless."

Concern overflowed...Andrew and Rachel must be terrified. "The children?"

Nathan rubbed my shoulder. "They slept through it. Margaret is with them. Your Uncle left to fetch the magistrate." He kissed my cheek, "All is well."

Nathan left my side and followed Mr. Carter downstairs, where Mr. Smith lay. I wondered at the desperation, the greed that would drive a man to madness. I was all but convinced he'd stolen from my father. But what now?

As Nathan had already mentioned, likely naught to be done about it. I wrestled in my mind the things that had happened. How close I'd come to losing my love. No matter how new, it would have been the deepest of losses, for I was convinced we'd enjoy the deepest of loves.

An hour passed, then another. I could not keep my eyes open. I did not know when Nathan opened the door to my room or when he slipped beside me. Only that when I woke, I'd slept in his arms, my head upon his chest.

Indeed, there was nowhere I'd rather be.

When I woke, he kissed me. "Merry Christmas, my love."

"Merry Christmas." I smiled up at him, still clothed in his shirt and trousers, absent the cravat I'd removed the night before. I blushed at the thought of what I'd done, of what I wanted.

Margaret brought a tray to my room. "Good morning," Her brow wrinkled with concern. "How do you fare after last night's shock?"

I leaned out of Nathan's arms, mindful that this was not at all decent. I spied the ring on my finger. And recalled what Uncle had told me. In God's eyes, we were not only decent but to relish the joy of our status.

"Don't mind me, dears. Don't mind me at all." She winked.

Christmas Eve passed with much napping between assisting in the kitchen and then, finally, attending midnight services at church.

Nathan and I stood side-by-side, with a child on either side of us, singing Adestes Fideles, Oh Come All Ye Faithful, Joyful and Triumphant.

We were triumphant. And we would indeed come to Him to sing adoration for how He was able to turn one man's greed into another man's noble gift.

Epilogue

Dearest Mother and Father,

Lord Sherborne delivered your message to me with all haste as you desired. He is a good gentleman, and I am quite glad to have made his and his wife's acquaintance. How kind of him to assist you in your legal matters, Father.

I am astounded that you should have recovered your fortune in its entirety in so short a time. How can this be? Will you stay with the Weatheringtons? Or resume your lives as before in Bath?

Please do not distress yourself on my behalf. As it is, your letter arrived too late, and I have already married Colonel Stewart. My pick of the men in London you say? I shan't, for I will have none other than this man I have married. There is none better than he, and though our time together has been short, I do indeed love him.

The children are dears, and I cannot wait for you to meet them. We shall pass by the Weatherington's in but one week.

Wish us joy. I miss you both.

Love,

Cassandra

Nathan put his arms around me. "You didn't open your Christmas present."

I spied an odd bundle by the hearth that wasn't there earlier. "What is it?"

"Something I believe you failed to pack when you began this adventure."

I couldn't think what. I slipped the ribbon away from the bundle and removed the paper. A seashell.

He kissed my cheek. "So you can hear the ocean when you miss it."

I wrapped my arms around him and never wanted to let go.

Ann Elizabeth Fryer loves nothing more than using story and romance to relay the depths and graciousness of a Father who holds us securely in the palms of His hands. Ann, her husband, and three children make their home in small-town Illinois where they can hear church bells keep time and tradition.

The Hearts Unlocked Collection:
Of Needles and Haystacks
Of Horse and Rider
Of Hearts and Home
Of Time and Circumstance
Of Pens and Ploughshares

Butterton Brides Series:
A Convenient Sacrifice
A Favorable Match
An Opportune Proposal
A Noble Gift

A Regency Hobbit Retelling:
An Unexpected Journey, coming November 28, 2024

Printed in Dunstable, United Kingdom